STUDENT BOOK

WorldView 4A

MICHAEL ROST

Araminta Crace **Robin Wileman**
Antonia Clare **JJ Wilson**

Simon Greenall
Series Editor, British English edition

WorldView Student Book 4A

Authorized adaptation from the United Kingdom edition entitled *Language to Go*, First Edition, published by Pearson Education Limited publishing under its Longman imprint.

American English adaptation: Ellen Shaw

American English adaptation published by Pearson Education, Inc. Copyright © 2005.

Pearson Education, 10 Bank Street, White Plains, NY 10606

Editorial director: Pamela Fishman
Development director: Irene Frankel
Senior development editor: José Antonio Méndez
Vice president, director of design and production: Rhea Banker
Executive managing editor: Linda Moser
Associate managing editors: Sandra Pike, Mike Kemper
Art director: Elizabeth Carlson
Vice president, director of international marketing: Bruno Paul
Senior manufacturing buyer: Edie Pullman
Text and cover design: Elizabeth Carlson
Photo research: Aerin Csigay
Text composition: Word and Image Design
Text font: 9.5/11pt Utopia and 9.5/11pt Frutiger Bold

ISBN: 0-13-184701-5

Library of Congress Control Number: 2003065959

Printed in the United States of America
3 4 5 6 7 8 9 10–BAM–09 08 07 06 05

Text Credits
Page **21** Somebody Already Broke My Heart. Words by Sade Adu. Music by Sade Adu, Stuart Matthewman, Andrew Hale, and Paul Spencer Denman. Copyright © 2000 Angel Music Ltd. All rights on behalf of Angel Music Ltd. in the United States administered by Sony/ATV Music Publishing, 8 Music Square West, Nashville, TN 37203. International copyright secured. All rights reserved; **59** Words Get in the Way by Gloria Estefan. Copyright © 2003 Foreign Imported Productions & Publishing, Inc. (BMI). International rights secured. All rights reserved. Used by permission.

Illustration Credits
Steve Attoe, pp. 22, 24, 56, 62; Brian Hughes, p. 47; Paul McCusker, p. 36; Susan Mogensen, p. 42.

Photo Credits
Page **2** *(middle)* DigitalVision/PictureQuest, *(top left)* Chris Baker/Getty Images, *(top right)* SuperStock/PictureQuest, *(bottom left)* Robert Dowling/Corbis, *(bottom right)* Royalty-Free/Corbis; **3** Lawrence Manning; **4** Jerome Tisne/Getty Images; **6** Trevor Clifford, *(hat & umbrella)* Dorling Kindersley Media Library; **7** Trevor Clifford, *(water)* Eric Fowke/PhotoEdit, *(bottom)* Powerstock Zefa; **9** Ray Juno/Corbis; **11** *(top)* Warren Webb/PhotoLibrary.com, *(middle)* Dorling Kindersley Media Library, *(bottom)* Getty Images; **12** Pat LaCroix/Getty Images; **14** Trevor Clifford; **15** Trevor Clifford, *(F)* Dorling Kindersley Media Library, *(G)* Dorling Kindersley Media Library; **16** Greg Pease/Getty Images; **18** *(top left)* Ryan McVay/Getty Images, *(top middle)* Amos Morgan/Getty Images, *(top right)* Nicolas Russell/Getty Images, *(right)* Willard Clay/Getty Images, *(bottom)* Mark Williams/Getty Images; **20** Eric Robert/Corbis; **25** M.Thomsen/Masterfile; **26** *(top)* Doug Pensinger/Getty Images, *(middle)* The Granger Collection, *(bottom)* Frederick M. Brown/Getty Images; **27** *(top)* Trevor Clifford, *(bottom)* AP/Wide World Photos; **28** Britt Erlanson/Getty Images; **30** *(top left)* Dorling Kindersley Media Library, *(top right)* Getty Images, *(bottom left)* Royalty-Free/Corbis, *(bottom right)* Frank La Bua/Pearson Education; **31** GDT; **32** Michael Newman/PhotoEdit; **34** *(A)* Adastra/Getty Images, *(B)* Dana White/PhotoEdit, *(C)* Christopher Bissell/Getty Images, *(D)* Stewart Cohen/Index Stock Imagery, *(E)* Dennis Nett/Syracuse Newspapers/The Image Works; *(F)* Susan Van Etten/PhotoEdit, *(G & H)* Spencer Grant/PhotoEdit, *(I & J)* Spencer Grant/PhotoEdit; **38** Rolex Awards/Tomas Bertelsen; **39** Matthew McVay/Corbis; **40** *(left)* Stockbyte/PictureQuest, *(right)* AP/Wide World Photos, *(bottom)* Warren Faidley/ImageState; **41** Todd Bigelow/Aurora & Quanta Productions Inc.; **43** Rudi Von Briel/PhotoEdit; **46** Ronnie Kaufman/Corbis; **48** Gareth Boden; **49** Gareth Boden; **50** David Young-Wolff/PhotoEdit; **54** *(top)* Britt Erlanson/Getty Images, *(bottom)* Getty Images; **58** Michael Putland/Retna Ltd.; **61** Kingfisher Challenges; **63** Digital Vision/Getty Images; **64** ImageState; **65** Katz Pictures/Antonio Pagnotta/Contrasto; **66** Robert Houser/Index Stock Imagery; **76** Derek Trask/Corbis.

Introduction

Welcome to *WorldView*, a four-level English course for adults and young adults. *WorldView* builds fluency by exploring a wide range of compelling topics presented from an international perspective. A trademark two-page lesson design, with clear and attainable language goals, ensures that students feel a sense of accomplishment and increased self-confidence in every class.

WorldView's approach to language learning follows a simple and proven **MAP**:

- **M**otivate learning through stimulating content and achievable learning goals.
- **A**nchor language production with strong, focused language presentations.
- **P**ersonalize learning through engaging and communicative speaking activities.

Course components

- **Student Book with Student Audio CD**
  The Student Book contains 28 four-page units; seven Review Units (one after every four units); four World of Music Units (two in each half of the book); Information for Pair and Group Work; a Vocabulary list; and a Grammar Reference section.

  The Student Audio CD includes tracks for all pronunciation and listening exercises in the *Student Book*. The Student Audio CD can be used with the *Student Book* for self-study and coordinates with the *Workbook* listening and pronunciation exercises.

- For each activity in the *Student Book*, the interleaved **Teacher's Edition** provides step-by-step procedures and exercise answer keys as well as a wealth of teacher support: unit Warm-ups, Optional Activities, Extensions, Culture Notes, Background Information, Teaching Tips, Wrap-ups, and extensive Language Notes. In addition, the *Teacher's Edition* includes a course orientation guide, full audio scripts, and the *Workbook* answer key.

- **The Workbook** has 28 four-page units that correspond to each of the *Student Book* units. Used in conjunction with the Student Audio CD, the *Workbook* provides abundant review and practice activities for Vocabulary, Grammar, Listening, Pronunciation, and Reading, along with Self-Quizzes after every four units. A Learning Strategies section at the beginning of the *Workbook* helps students to be active learners.

- **The Class Audio Program** is available in either CD or cassette format and contains all the recorded material for in-class use.

- **The Teacher's Resource Book** (with **Testing Audio CD** and **TestGen Software**) has three sections of reproducible material: extra communication activities for in-class use, model writing passages for each *Student Book* writing assignment, and a complete testing program: seven quizzes and two tests, along with scoring guides and answer keys. Also included are an Audio CD for use with the quizzes and tests and an easy-to-use TestGen software CD for customizing the tests.

- For each level of the course, the ***WorldView* Video** presents seven, five-minute authentic video segments connected to *Student Book* topics. Notes to the Teacher are available in the Video package, and Student Activity Sheets can be downloaded from the ***WorldView* Companion Website**.

- **The *WorldView* Companion Website** (www.longman.com/worldview) provides a variety of teaching support, including Video Activity Sheets and supplemental vocabulary material.

Unit contents

Each of the 28 units in *WorldView* has seven closely linked sections:

- **Getting started:** a communicative opening exercise that introduces target vocabulary
- **Listening:** an authentic-sounding conversation, radio interview, narration, etc., that introduces target grammar
- **Reading:** a magazine article, book excerpt, questionnaire, etc., that introduces target grammar
- **Grammar focus:** an exercise sequence that allows students to focus on the new grammar point and to solidify their learning
- **Pronunciation:** stress, rhythm, and intonation practice based on the target vocabulary and grammar
- **Speaking:** an interactive speaking task focused on student production of target vocabulary, grammar, and functional language
- **Writing:** a personalized writing activity that stimulates student production of target vocabulary and grammar
- **Conversation to go:** a concise reminder of the grammar and functional language introduced in the unit

Course length

With its flexible format and course components, *WorldView* responds to a variety of course needs, and is suitable for 70 to 90 hours of classroom instruction. Each unit can be easily expanded by using bonus activities from the *Teacher's Edition*, reproducible activities available in the *Teacher's Resource Book*, linked lessons from the *WorldView* Video program, and supplementary vocabulary assignments in the *WorldView* Companion Website.

The *WorldView Student Book* with Student Audio CD and the *Workbook* are also available in split editions.

Scope and Sequence

GRAMMAR FOCUS	PRONUNCIATION	SPEAKING	WRITING
Present perfect with *yet, already, just*	Falling and rising intonation in questions	Describing changes in your life	Write a letter about changes in your life
Real conditional	Stress in compound nouns	Making suggestions	Write an article for a travel magazine
Count/non-count nouns and quantifiers	Reduction of unstressed words	Describing how to make a dish	Write about what you eat on a typical day
Modals: *will, may, might, could* for prediction and speculation	Sentence stress: pitch changes around focus words	Making predictions about advances in technology	Describe a futuristic invention
Modals: *may, can, could, Is it OK if? / Do you mind if? / Would you mind if?* for permission	Intonation in polite requests	Asking for and giving/refusing permission	Write about polite customs and explain why they are important
Present perfect and present perfect continuous	Weak and contracted forms of *have* and *has*	Discussing personal achievements and ongoing activities	Write an application letter
Expressions of purpose: *to, in order to, so that, for*	Stress patterns in words	Describing reasons for doing things	Write an email about security measures in the workplace and their consequences
Past perfect	Weak and contracted forms of *had*	Talking about events in your life	Describe an interesting experience
Indirect statements	The *th* sounds: /ð/ (weather) and /θ/ (thick)	Reporting on what you hear or read	Write an email describing the weather and making predictions
Simple future and future perfect	Contracted and weak forms of *will* and *have*	Predicting future events	Write a diary entry about future plans
Indirect questions	Consonant clusters	Reporting a conversation or interview	Write a letter recounting a conversation or interview
Narrative past tenses: simple past, past continuous, past perfect, past perfect continuous	Main stress in sentences	Telling stories in the past	Write a story about important events in your past
Present unreal conditional	Weak and contracted forms of *would* and weak pronunciation of *could*	Talking about hypothetical situations	Write about an extreme, hypothetical situation
Connectors: *although, despite (not), however, in spite of*	Phrase groups and intonation	Comparing attitudes toward life situations	Describe daily routines related to commuting

UNIT 1

Changes

Vocabulary Words related to lifestyles
Grammar Present perfect with *yet, already, just*
Speaking Describing changes in your life

Lesson **A**

Getting started

1 **Which of these do you have in your life right now? Check (✓) them.**

clutter ___	contentment ___	energy ___
good health ___	good luck ___	happiness ___
productivity ___	stress ___	success ___
tension ___	tranquility ___	wealth ___

2 *PAIRS.* **Answer these questions about the things in Exercise 1.**

Which things would you like to have more of or less of?
Which are the three most important things for you?
Can we do anything to change things? If so, what can we do?

3 *PAIRS.* **Write the adjective form for the nouns in Exercise 1.**

clutter—cluttered

4 🎧 **Listen and check your answers. Then listen and repeat.**

Reading

5 **Have you ever heard of Feng Shui? Where do you think it comes from?**

6 **Read the article about Feng Shui and answer these questions.**

1. What does the article say you should do every day?
2. What does the article say about colors?

Want to change your life but don't know how?

Is Feng Shui the answer?

Feng Shui is an ancient Chinese philosophy for a healthy, happy, and successful lifestyle that will make you more content with your life. Read on for some advice.

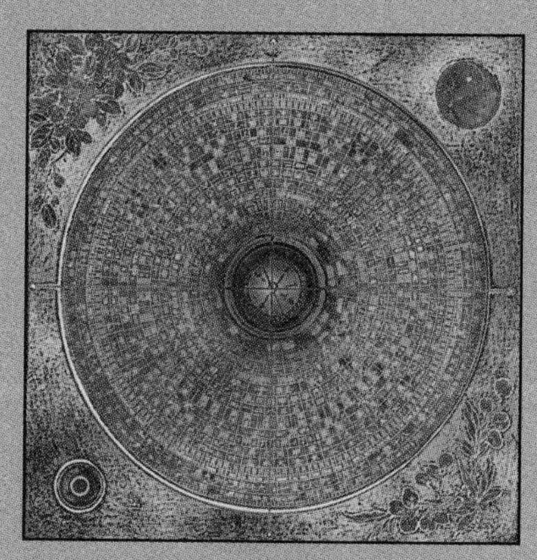

Chart used for setting up Feng Shui.

- Take up a sport or start going for a walk every day. Make sure you get some fresh air during the day.
- Start your day with a glass of water. You'll feel more energetic.
- Buy a fish tank. Fish are considered lucky, so you may even become wealthy!
- Clean up your home and workplace every day.
- Use plants to create a calm and tranquil atmosphere at home or at work.
- Don't wear gray clothes. Gray is neither black nor white; it's a sign of confusion.
- Try to avoid stressful or tense situations and places, like crowded streets and noisy traffic.

Remember: With Feng Shui, you don't predict the future. You change it.

7 *PAIRS.* **Discuss. Do you think Feng Shui works? Would you like to try it?**

Listening

8 **Listen to the interview with Bill Costa, who has tried Feng Shui. In the article on Feng Shui, check (✓) the advice that Bill has followed.**

9 **Listen again. Write *T* (true) or *F* (false) after each statement.**

1. Feng Shui has changed Bill's life.
2. Bill has started running recently.
3. He believes that the fish have brought him good luck.

Grammar focus

1 **Study the examples of the present perfect with *yet, already,* and *just*.**

Have you **bought** any fish **yet**?
I **haven't started** on the house **yet**.
I**'ve tried** one or two of the ideas **already**.
I**'ve already cleaned** up my desk.
I**'ve just bought** myself a new blue suit.

2 **Look at the examples again. Complete the rules in the chart with *yet, already,* or *just*.**

Present perfect with *yet, already,* and *just*
Use ________ when something hasn't happened, but you expect it to happen in the future.
Use ________ when something has happened very recently.
Use ________ when something has happened sooner than expected.
Use ________ in questions and negative sentences.
________ always goes between *have* and the past participle.
________ goes at the end of a clause.
________ can go either between *have* and the past participle or at the end of the clause.

Grammar Reference page 142

3 **Write sentences in the present perfect using the cues. Use *yet, already,* and *just* where appropriate.**

1. My neighbor works out every day. (She / start training for the marathon)
   She's just started training for the marathon.
2. Kumiko works really fast. (She / do her homework)
3. What's the weather like this morning? (You / be outside?)
4. (My neighbor / redecorate / his living room) It looks great!
5. I don't know where I'm going on vacation. (I / not decided)
6. (I / finish reading a book on Feng Shui) It's very interesting.
7. Rogelio had to be home early today. (He / leave)
8. I don't want to watch that movie on TV. (I / see it)
9. Are you hungry? (You / have lunch?)
10. I'm so happy. (I / find a job) I start next week.

Pronunciation

4 **Listen. Notice the way the intonation changes on the focus word (the most important word). The intonation then goes up at the end of the *Yes/No* questions and down at the end of the *Wh-* questions.**

Has your life **changed** yet?

What **chang**es have you made in your life?

How about straightening up your **work**place?

Have you bought any **fish** yet?

5 **Listen again and repeat.**

Speaking

6 *BEFORE YOU SPEAK.* **Think about recent changes in your life—in your home, work, family, leisure activities, or personal appearance. Make notes on two or three changes you have already made, and one or two changes you plan to make.**

Already done	Not done yet
joined a gym	started working out

7 *GROUPS OF 4.* **Take turns. Ask each other questions about the changes in your lives.**

A: What changes have you made in your life recently?
B: Well, I've just joined a gym.
C: Really? And how often do you go?

Writing

8 **Write a short letter to a friend. Tell your friend about recent changes in your life. What have you done and what haven't you done yet to make these changes?**

CONVERSATION TO GO

A: **Have** you **finished** moving in **yet**?
B: No, Mother, we just got here. We **haven't unpacked** a thing **yet**! No, you can't come for dinner!

UNIT 2

Australia

Vocabulary Travel items
Grammar Real conditional
Speaking Making suggestions

Lesson A

Getting started

1 *PAIRS.* **Think of things you might take on a camping trip. Match the words on the left with the words on the right to make compound nouns.**

1. first-aid kit______	gear
2. hiking ________	guide
3. insect ________	belt
4. money ________	bottle
5. rain ________	bag
6. sleeping ________	boots
7. travel ________	repellent
8. water ________	~~kit~~

2 **Look at the pictures of the travel items. Label them with the words in Exercise 1.**

Pronunciation

3 **Listen to the words in Exercise 1. Which syllable is stressed in a compound noun?**

4 **Listen again and repeat.**

5 *PAIRS* **Which of the travel items from Exercise 1 would you take on a . . .**

- two-week vacation at the beach?
- trip to the mountains?
- weekend visit to a big city?

F_1

G___

H___

Listening

6 🎧 **Jeff is packing for a weekend trip. Listen to his conversation with his roommate. Look at the pictures and check (✓) the things Jeff is taking.**

Reading

7 **Look at the picture of the Australian Outback and answer these questions.**

Do you know anyone who has been to Australia?

What do you know about it?

8 **Read the article about the Australian Outback and answer these questions.**

1. What's the best way to travel around the Outback?
2. When is the best time to go?
3. What wildlife can you see?
4. What outdoor activities are there?
5. What health risks are there?

9 *PAIRS.* **Compare your answers.**

The Australian Outback

The Outback is huge—it's 1,878 miles (3,022 km) from Adelaide to Darwin. So, unless you have a lot of time, you'll find that flights and rental cars are the best ways to travel. It will be cheaper to buy a pass if you plan to take several flights.

Unless you like extremely hot weather, avoid December and January, when the temperature can go up to 40°C (104°F). If you go in July and August, it won't be too hot during the day, but the nights will be freezing. The best times to visit are April to June and October to November. If you visit Kakadu's wetlands in the dry season, you'll see thousands of crocodiles.

And if you want to see kangaroos, look for them in the mornings and evenings. You may even see dingoes—if you're very lucky.

If you like outdoor activities, you can go canoeing up Katherine Gorge or ride camels at Uluru. One of the best ways to see the Outback is to walk. Wear boots if you go walking—Australia has the most dangerous snakes in the world. The sun is very strong for most of the year, so you should use high-SPF sunscreen and wear a hat. You should also carry plenty of water with you. If you want to go camping, you'll find that many tour companies offer camping trips.

Grammar focus

1 **Study the examples of the real conditional. Notice that each sentence has two parts: an *if* clause and a result clause.**

> It **will be** cheaper to buy a pass **if** you **plan** to take several flights.
> **If** you**'re going** hiking, you**'ll need** some insect repellent.
> **If** you **like** outdoor activities, you **can go** canoeing up Katherine Gorge.
> **If** you **go** in July or August, it **won't be** too hot.
> **Unless** you **like** extremely hot weather, **avoid** December and January.

2 **Look at the examples again. Complete the rules in the chart with *if* or *result*.**

Real conditional
Use the real conditional to talk about future possibilities. The __________ clause states the condition. Use the simple present tense in the __________ clause. Use the future with *will* or *be going to*, a modal, or an imperative in the __________ clause.
NOTE: *Unless* can sometimes be used in place of *if . . . not.*

Grammar Reference page 142

3 **Combine the beginnings of the sentences on the left with the endings on the right to make conditional sentences. Use *if* or *unless* as appropriate.**

Take a water bottle if you want safe drinking water.

1. Take a water bottle
2. You'll need to wear boots
3. You may see fantastic sunrises
4. You'll need to take rain gear
5. Find a tour company offering adventure sports
6. You'll need to use sunscreen
7. You may not get tickets for the flights
8. You'll get lost

a. you make your reservations in advance.
b. you don't want to get sunburned.
c. you want to go canoeing.
d. you go hiking.
e. you use a very good map.
~~f.~~ you want safe drinking water.
g. you go in the dry season.
h. you get up early.

Speaking

4 *BEFORE YOU SPEAK.* **Think about a tourist destination in your country or any place you know. Make notes about your chosen place.**

5 *PAIRS.* **Role-play. Student A, you're a travel agent giving suggestions and information to Student B. Student B, you're a tourist. You want to go to the place Student A chose in Exercise 4. Ask Student A questions about the place. Then switch roles.**

B: Hi. I'd like some information about British Columbia, Canada.
A: Sure. What do you want to know?
B: When is the best time to go there?
A: If you go in June, you'll have very nice weather.

6 **Report to the class. What have you learned about the place your partner chose?**

Writing

7 **Write a short article for a travel magazine describing a vacation place that you know. Use the real conditional.**

CONVERSATION TO GO

A: When is the best time to go?
B: If you go in the winter, you'll avoid the crowds.

What's cooking?

Vocabulary Cooking terms and ingredients
Grammar Count/non-count nouns and quantifiers
Speaking Describing how to make a dish

Lesson A

Getting started

1 *PAIRS.* **Discuss these questions.**

How often do you cook?
What is your favorite type of food?

2 *PAIRS.* **Match the words in the box with their definitions.**

a. add	b. (bring to a) boil	c. broil	d. chop	e. melt	f. mix
g. pour	h. sauté	i. serve	j. simmer	k. soak	l. stir

1. Put one ingredient in with another __a__
2. Cook quickly in a little hot oil or fat ____
3. Turn solid food into liquid by heating it ____
4. Present a finished meal, ready for eating ____
5. Cook in very hot water ____
6. Cover with liquid for a period of time ____
7. Cut into small uneven pieces ____
8. Combine different ingredients together ____
9. Cook meat, fish, etc., over or under direct heat ____
10. Move a liquid or food with a spoon in order to mix it ____
11. Cook slowly in liquid over low heat ____
12. Make liquid flow steadily from a container ____

Listening

3 **Listen to the cooking show, *Now We're Cooking*, and look at the pictures. Which group of ingredients is for the first recipe?**

Ⓐ

Ⓑ

4 Listen to the chef's recipes and complete the sentences.

Chile con carne

1. Boil the kidney beans for 10 minutes.
2. ______ the onions and the beef until the beef turns brown.
3. Add the tomato paste, the chopped ______, and the kidney beans.
4. Let the chili con carne ______ for 30 minutes.
5. ______ with rice.

Cajun shrimp

1. Let the sauce ______ for about an hour.
2. ______ most of the butter in a large saucepan.
3. Cook the ______ for 2 minutes, before adding the rest of the butter.
4. Add the rest of the butter and the ______.
5. Serve with ______.

Reading

5 Have you ever heard of the Mediterranean diet? What do you think it is?

6 Read the article. Complete the chart to describe what people eat on the Mediterranean diet.

A little	red meat
A lot	
Some	

7 *PAIRS.* **Discuss these questions.**

Is your diet similar to the Mediterranean diet, or is it very different?

Do you think you would like the Mediterranean diet? Why?

The Mediterranean Diet

The Mediterranean diet comes from a number of different countries bordering the Mediterranean Sea, including Greece, southern Italy, Portugal, and southern Spain. People who follow this diet generally live longer, and very few get heart disease.

Mediterranean people eat a lot of fruit, vegetables, grains, beans, and nuts on a regular basis. They use a great deal of olive oil. They don't eat much butter, but they do have some dairy products, including milk. People from this region eat fish and poultry a few times a week. However, the diet does not include a great deal of red meat. People from the Mediterranean region also drink a small amount of wine with a meal, which according to several studies, has some health benefits.

Many people in non-Mediterranean countries have switched to the Mediterranean diet because it is not only a healthful way of eating, but an enjoyable one.

3

Lesson B

Grammar focus

1 **Look at the examples. Are the words in italics count or non-count nouns? Write *C* or *NC* next to each sentence. Notice the quantifiers before count and non-count nouns.**

Heat a little *oil* in a saucepan.
Chop several *onions*.

2 **Look at the examples again and the article on page 11. Write the quantifiers in the correct columns in the chart.**

a few C, much NC, few C, all, a number of C, some, most of, each C, a little bit of NC, a great deal of NC, plenty of NC, many C, a lot of, a little NC, several C

Count/Non-count nouns and quantifiers		
Count nouns only	**Non-count nouns only**	**Both**
a few		

Grammar Reference page 142

3 **Underline the correct quantifiers.**

1. **a few / a little** herbs
2. **each / all** the onions
3. **a little / a few** salt and pepper
4. **a lot of / several** tomato paste
5. **most of / many of** the butter
6. **a large number of / plenty of** vegetable oil
7. **several / some** chili powder
8. **a little bit of / a few** chicken stock
9. **a little / a small number of** chili powder
10. **not too many / not too much** milk
11. **not a great deal of / not a large number of** chili powder
12. **much / several** eggs

Pronunciation

4 **Listen. Notice the pronunciation of the words *a*, *and*, *of*, *in*, and *some*. Are these words stressed? Why?**

a clove of garlic	Chop a clove of garlic.
some oil	Heat some oil in a pan.
salt and pepper	Add a little salt and pepper.
a lot of	Don't use a lot of chili powder.

5 **Listen again and repeat.**

Speaking

6 *BEFORE YOU SPEAK.* **Think of a dish you know how to cook. Make notes on the ingredients and procedure for cooking.**

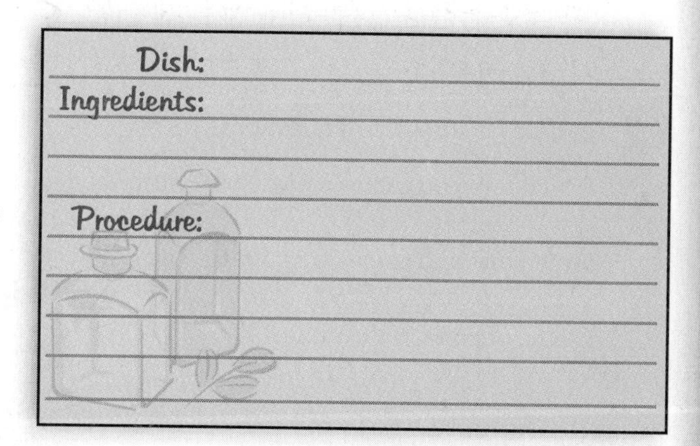

7 *PAIRS.* **Take turns explaining how to make your dish. Ask and answer questions about ingredients and procedures. Take notes on your partner's recipe.**

A: For this pasta dish, we need macaroni, chicken stock, onions, tomatoes . . .

B: How much macaroni do we need?

A: One box of macaroni and a lot of chicken stock—about four cups. We need several onions and tomatoes . . .

8 **Tell the class about your partner's dish. Would you like to try it?**

Writing

9 **Write about what you eat on a typical day. Be as specific as you can. As appropriate, use quantifiers with count and non-count nouns.**

CONVERSATION TO GO

A: What ingredients will I need to make this dish?
B: **Several** large eggs, **some** butter, **a little bit of** garlic, and **a little** salt.

UNIT 4

Toys of the future

Vocabulary Toys and games
Grammar Modals: *will, may, might, could* for prediction and speculation
Speaking Making predictions

Lesson A

Getting started

1 *PAIRS.* **Match the words in the box with the pictures.**

1. action figure ___	6. handheld video game ___
2. board game ___	7. jigsaw puzzle ___
3. cards ___	8. remote-controlled car ___
4. doll ___	9. skateboard ___
5. erector set truck ___	10. stuffed animal ___

2 *PAIRS.* **Discuss these questions.**

Which toys and games did you play with when you were a child?

Which toys and games are popular with adults?

What kinds of toys and games do you think will be popular in the future?

Listening

3 **Listen to the radio interview. Which of the following are discussed in the interview? Circle the letters.**

a. dolls b. virtual child
c. toy robots d. emotionally sensitive toys

4 **Listen again. Answer the questions. Use the choices in Exercise 3.**

1. Which toy will be able to create a computer image of a real toy?
2. Which toys will be able to tell your mood?
3. Which toys will be able to talk to people?

5 *PAIRS.* **Discuss. Do you think the dolls of the future might be good for children? Why?**

A B C D

Tomorrow's Toys

In the future, toys will give us excitement, entertainment, and wonderful learning opportunities. What kinds of toys can we expect to see?

6. **Look at the article "Tomorrow's Toys." Look at the names of the six toys. Without reading the descriptions, guess what these toys will be like.**

7. **Read the article quickly to see if your guesses in Exercise 6 were correct.**

8. **Read the article again. Write *T* (true) or *F* (false) after each statement.**

   1. Some toys will protect children from traffic dangers.
   2. Some toys will talk to people.
   3. Some toys will teach people new languages.
   4. Ludic Robots® will be able to follow some orders.
   5. Soccer balls of the future might cause arguments.
   6. The hover skateboard will move on wheels.

E F

The Navigator Game® will connect to a child's bicycle. This small gadget will use communication technology to link children together. Children will be able to communicate and play simple games, such as hide-and-seek, using a radio signal. The radio signal will also warn children of approaching cars.

Ludic Robots® are small, electronic friends that respond to voice commands, touch, and gestures. They can also be taught to do simple tasks, so children may become very fond of them.

Soccer balls of the future might contain video cameras. These cameras could show exactly where the ball is, so arguments about goals might become a thing of the past.

The Interactive Globe® will show lots of information about the world, such as different time zones, the world's languages, and the weather around the world. When not in use, the Globe could be used as a night-light.

Interactive Books® will grow up with their readers, taking them from simple story-telling with pictures through learning to read. Readers will use a touch screen to choose voices and faces for their characters and create their own pictures, making the stories more personal.

The hover skateboard could become available in a few years. It will look almost like a regular skateboard, but instead of moving on wheels, it will glide on a cushion of air.

Grammar focus

1 **Study the examples with *will, may, might,* and *could* for prediction and speculation.**

> I'm sure little girls **will** still play with dolls.
> Children **may** become very fond of the Ludic Robots.
> The Globe **could** be used as a night-light.
> I think some children **might** want a virtual friend.

2 **Look at the examples again. Complete the rules in the chart with *will, may, might,* or *could.***

Modals: *will, may, might, could* for prediction and speculation
Use __________ to express a future event that is very likely to happen. Use __________, __________, and __________ to express a future event that is possible, but less likely, to happen.
NOTE: Use *will, may, might,* or *could* after *I think.* Use *will* after *I'm sure, I don't think / I doubt if, I expect.*

Grammar Reference page 143

3 **Write sentences about the future using the cues. Use *will, may, might, could,* or *won't.* Some items may have more than one answer.**

1. I think / computer graphics / become / very realistic (very likely)
   I think computer graphics will become very realistic.
2. In the future / more children / play indoors / all the time (possibly)
3. I'm sure / people / not read / printed books much longer (very likely)
4. Personal flying machines / become / available / by the year 2020 (possibly)
5. I expect / most children / have / cell phones and pagers / before long (very likely)
6. Very soon / I think / famous people / be / characters in computer games (very likely)
7. Skateboards / have / electric motors / soon (possibly)
8. I expect / stuffed animals / not be / very popular much longer (very likely)
9. Digitally created characters / replace human actors in movies (possibly)

4 *GROUPS OF 3.* **Which of the sentences in Exercise 3 do you agree with?**

Pronunciation

5 **Long sentences are often divided into thought groups. Listen. Notice the way the focus word (the most important word) in each sentence or thought group stands out. The voice jumps up or down on this word and the vowel sound is long and clear.**

I'm **sure** / little girls will play with **dolls.**/

I ex**pect** / they'll have dis**cus**sions with their dolls. /

Do you **real**ly think/ dolls will **talk** to people?/

I'm **sure** they will. /

Do you **think** / this could happen anytime **soon**?/

It **might** happen / sooner than we **think**. /

6 **Listen again and repeat.**

Speaking

7 *BEFORE YOU SPEAK.* **Think about these kinds of products. What do you think they will be like in the future? Make notes about your predictions.**

Toys — small, have computers in them

Video and computer games

Other kinds of technology

8 *PAIRS.* **Take turns asking and answering questions about your predictions. Use these expressions in your answers:**

- I think
- I don't think
- I expect
- I doubt if
- I'm sure

A: What do you think the toys of the future will be like?
B: I'm sure that a lot of toys will have computers in them.

Writing

9 **Think of a product for the future that you'd like to have, for example, a toy, an appliance, or a car. Write a description of this product for a catalog.**

Conversation to go

A: **Do you think** life **will** get better in the future?
B: I can't say, but **I know it'll be** different!

Review 1 Units 1–4

Unit 1 Changes

1 *PAIRS.* Listen to three people talking about changes they are making in their lives. Discuss what each person has done so far and what he or she plans to do.

A Roberto

B Tao

C Alex

2 *PAIRS.* Choose one of these projects or another project of your own. Tell your partner. Your partner will ask questions about what you have done to reach your goals. Take turns.

- clean up or redecorate the house
- get a good (or better) job
- get in shape
- improve your English
- play a sport really well
- find a boyfriend/girlfriend

Unit 2 Australia

3 *PAIRS.* Look at the pictures and discuss these questions.

Have you ever been to these places?
What do you know about them?
Would you like to go to either one?

4 *PAIRS.* Role-play a travel agent and a traveler who wants to visit one of the places in the pictures. Ask and answer questions. Then switch roles.

Student A, look at page 136.
Student B, look at page 138.

Colorado, USA

Bangkok, Thailand

Unit 3 What's cooking?

5 *PAIRS.* Look at a recipe for one minute and try to remember the ingredients and procedure. Don't look at your partner's recipe.

Student A, look at page 136. Student B, look at page 138.

6 *PAIRS.* Take turns telling your partner how to make your "dish" but don't say what it is. Your partner guesses what it is. Ask and answer follow-up questions.

A: *First break some eggs.*
B: *How many?*

7 *PAIRS.* Follow the same directions from Exercise 6 for another recipe that you know how to prepare.

Unit 4 Toys of the future

8 Listen to the radio interview with a futurologist. Do you agree with his predictions?

9 *GROUPS OF 4.* Make predictions as a group for changes you think will or might happen 20 years in the future. Discuss the following ideas and others of your own.

Topic	Possibilities	Agree or Disagree?
Money	Electronic cash? World currency?	
Electronic shopping	Everyone will use it? Some won't?	
TVs/video	Video walls? 3-D TVs and video games?	
Robots	Will do all the housework? Might be lovable?	
Energy	Will cost more? Could cost less?	
Other ideas		

10 Share your opinions with the rest of the class.

World of Music 1

Somebody Already Broke My Heart

Sade

Vocabulary

1 **Match the words in bold with the correct definitions.**

1. My friends are always there to **pull** me **through** a crisis. c
2. It **tears** me **apart** when I see someone in pain. ___
3. I can always **count on** my family to help me. ___
4. I was once **stranded** at the airport without any money. ___
5. We all need a **savior** at some point in our lives. ___

a. depend or rely on something or someone
b. needing help because you are unable to move from a place or situation
c. help someone survive after a difficult or upsetting situation
d. someone or something that saves you from a difficult situation
e. make someone extremely unhappy or upset

2 *PAIRS.* **Choose one verb or verb phrase from Exercise 1 to talk about a personal experience.**

*Born Helen Folasade Adu in 1959, pop and rock star **Sade** spent her early years in Nigeria and then moved to England. She started in the music world as a songwriter to later become a singer. Her hits include "Smooth Operator" and "Love Is Stronger Than Pride."*

Listening

3 **Listen to "Somebody Already Broke My Heart" by Sade. How does the singer feel? Circle the answer.**

a. She has found someone to love, but she's afraid of being hurt again.
b. She doesn't want to fall in love ever again.
c. She is afraid that she will hurt the new person in her life.

4 **Listen to the song again and complete the lyrics on page 21.**

Somebody Already Broke My Heart

You came along when I needed a savior
Someone to pull me through somehow
_____ _____ _____ apart so many times
_____ _____ _____ so many times before
So I'm counting on you now

Somebody already broke my heart
Somebody already broke my heart

Here I am
So don't leave me stranded
On the end of a line
Hanging on the edge of a lie
_____ _____ _____ apart so many times
_____ _____ _____ so many times before
So be careful and be kind

Somebody already broke my heart
If someone _____ _____ lose,
I _____ _____ _____ play
Somebody already broke my heart
No, no I can't go there again

You came along when I needed a savior
Someone to pull me through somehow
_____ _____ _____ apart so many times
_____ _____ _____ so many times before
So I'm counting on you now

Somebody already broke my heart
If someone _____ _____ lose,
I _____ _____ _____ play
Somebody already broke my heart
No, no I can't go there again

Speaking

5 *GROUPS OF 3.* **Discuss these questions. Use lines from the song to explain your answers.**

1. Look at the first stanza. The singer says she needed a "savior." Why did she need to be saved?
2. How does the singer ask the new person in her life to behave?

How rude!

Vocabulary Manners and polite customs
Grammar Modals: *may, can, could,* and *Is it OK if . . . ?/Do you mind if . . . ?/ Would you mind if . . . ?* for permission
Speaking Asking for and giving/refusing permission

Lesson **A**

Getting started 

1 *PAIRS.* **Look at the picture and answer these questions.**

1. Who is snapping his/her fingers?
2. Who has his/her elbows on the table?
3. Who is slurping while eating?
4. Who is reaching across the table?
5. Who is pointing at someone?
6. Who is eating with his or her fingers?
7. Who is blowing his or her nose?
8. Who has his or her feet up on the chair?

2 *GROUPS OF 3.* **Discuss. Which of the behaviors in the picture are rude in your country?**

Reading

3 *PAIRS.* **How much do you know about good manners in the United States? Take the quiz. Check (✓) *T* (true) or *F* (false) after each statement.**

Minding Your Manners in the United States

Did you know that good manners are cultural? In other words, what's all right to do in one country may not be appropriate in another country. See how much you know about what's OK and what's not OK in the United States.

	T	F
1. It's impolite to ask people how much money they make.	○	○
2. It's OK to interrupt other people while they are talking.	○	○
3. When someone invites you to a restaurant, it's OK to offer to pay for your meal.	○	○
4. It's impolite to put your elbows on the table at mealtimes.	○	○
5. When people invite you to their house for dinner, it's impolite to be a few minutes early.	○	○
6. When you are at a friend's house, it's OK to use your friend's telephone without asking.	○	○
7. In a restaurant, it's OK to snap your fingers when you want to call the server.	○	○
8. It's very rude to eat when you are walking down the street.	○	○
9. It's impolite to point your finger at another person.	○	○
10. It's impolite to smoke in a public place without asking.	○	○
11. It's impolite to open a present in front of the person who gave it to you.	○	○
12. It's very rude to give money as a wedding present.	○	○

Check your answers on page 140.

4 *GROUPS OF 4.* **Were you surprised by any of the answers? Are the answers the same for your country?**

Listening

5 **Listen and match the conversations with the general situations described in the quiz in Exercise 3.**

a. 6 b. 7 c. 3 d. 10 e. 1 f. 2 g. 5

Grammar focus

1 **Study the examples. Notice the ways to ask for permission and the ways to respond.**

Asking permission	Giving permission	Refusing permission
May I take care of the tip? **Can** I pay for my share?	**Sure. Why not?**	**Oh, no.** You're my guest.
Could I use your phone, please?	**Yes, of course.**	**Sorry, but** I'm expecting a call.
Is it OK if I use the fax?	**Sure, go ahead.**	**No, sorry.** It's not working right now.
Do you mind if I smoke?	**No, I don't mind.**	**I'm sorry, but** smoking is not allowed.
Would you mind if sat here?	**No, not at all.**	**I'm sorry, but** this seat is taken.

2 **Look at the examples again. Underline the correct information to complete the rules in the chart.**

Modals: *may, can, could,* and *Is it OK if . . . ? / Do you mind if . . . ? / Would you mind if . . . ?* for permission
After *may, can,* and *could*, use the **base form of the verb / infinitive**.
After *Is it OK if* + subject and *Do you mind if* + subject, use the **base form / simple present form** of the verb.
After *Would you mind if* + subject, use the **simple present / simple past** form of the verb.
To give permission to questions beginning with *Do you mind* or *Would you mind*, say **yes / no**.

Grammar Reference page 143

3 **Write conversations using the cues. Be sure to give a reason when you refuse.**

1. A: I want to open the window. (do/mind)
   B: (agree)

   A: Do you mind if I open the window?
   B: No, not at all.

2. A: I want to give you some advice. (may)
   B: (agree)
3. A: I'd like to use your pencil. (could)
   B: (agree)
4. A: I need to borrow your dictionary. (can)
   B: (refuse)
5. A: We want to sit here. (OK)
   B: (refuse)
6. A: I'd like to use your computer. (would/mind)
   B: (agree)
7. A: I'd like to call you sometime. (could)
   B: (agree)
8. A: I want to leave work early today. (would/mind)
   B: (refuse)

Pronunciation

4 **Listen. Notice the rising intonation in these polite questions.**

May we have the **check**, please? Is it OK if I leave **early**?

Do you mind if I come **in**? Would you mind if I asked you a **question**?

5 **Listen to these questions. You will hear each question twice. Which intonation sounds more polite, *a* or *b*?**

1. Could I use your phone? b
2. Is it OK if I close the window? a
3. Do you mind if I sit here? a
4. Can I look at your newspaper? b

6 **Listen and repeat the polite questions.**

Speaking

7 *PAIRS.* **Take turns asking for permission and responding.**

Student A: look at page 139. Read the situations.
Student B: look at page 141. Respond to Student A.

A: Can I use your computer?
B: I'm sorry, but I need it to do my homework.

8 **Switch roles.**

Student B: look at page 141. Read the situations.
Student A: look at page 139. Respond to Student B.

Writing

9 **Think of two or three important polite ways in your country for making requests or asking permission. Describe what those customs mean and explain why it is important to use them in your culture.**

Conversation to Go

A: **Could I borrow** your car?
B: **I'm sorry.** I need it tonight.
A: Well, **is it OK if I use your phone** to call a taxi?

Achievement

Vocabulary Verbs related to achievements and projects
Grammar Present perfect and present perfect continuous
Speaking Discussing personal achievements and projects

Lesson **A**

Getting started

1 *PAIRS.* **Match the verbs with the correct nouns to make expressions related to achievements.**

Verbs	Nouns
1. achieve ___	a. an obstacle / a problem
2. come up with ___	b. a certificate / an award
3. develop ___	c. a race / a prize
4. invent ___	d. a skill / a plan
5. overcome ___	e. a machine / a device
6. pass ___	f. a goal / an objective
7. receive ___	g. an idea / a solution
8. solve ___	h. an exam / a course
9. win ___	i. a problem / a puzzle

2 *PAIRS.* **Complete the sentences with the correct form of the verbs in Exercise 1. You will not need all the verbs.**

1. Lance Armstrong tied the Tour de France record when he ___won___ the race for the fifth time.
2. Albert Einstein ___________ the theory of relativity, an idea that changed physics forever.
3. After she left Destiny's Child, Beyonce ___________ numerous awards, including five Grammies in 2004.
4. Airline pilots have to ___________ rigorous exams to keep their jobs.
5. After many years of hard work, David Beckham ___________ his goal of becoming a soccer star.
6. Of all the devices that people have ever ___________, the steam engine is the most far-reaching.
7. Imagination is the capacity to ___________ a problem you have never had before.

3 *GROUPS OF 4.* **Choose two phrases from Exercise 1. Make sentences about yourself or people you know. Take turns sharing your sentence. Ask and answer follow-up questions.**

My friend at work came up with a great idea for a new video game.

Listening

4 🎧 **Listen to the radio program about Trevor Baylis, an inventor. Which of the three radios did Trevor Baylis invent? Check (✓) the correct picture.**

A___ B___ C___

5 🎧 **Listen again and answer these questions.**

1. Why did Trevor invent the windup radio?
2. What else has he invented?
3. What is he working on and developing currently?

Reading

6 **Look at the picture of a new invention called the IBOT™. What do you think it will be able to do?**

7 **Read the article. Was your answer in Exercise 6 correct?**

8 **Read the article again and answer these questions.**

1. How is the IBOT different from ordinary wheelchairs?
2. Why did Kamen come up with the idea of improving the wheelchair?
3. How did he start to develop the technology for his invention?
4. What makes him want to work on a new project?

Reinventing the Wheelchair

Have you ever heard the phrase "confined to a wheelchair"? The phrase is often used to refer to people using wheelchairs. But inventor Dean Kamen thinks wheelchairs should help physically impaired people become free. He has come up with a design for a revolutionary new wheelchair called the IBOT™, or the Independence IBOT™ Mobility System.

Kamen's invention promises to improve the way many people live. The IBOT™ will go almost anywhere, climb up and down stairs, and even raise itself up to reach top shelves.

For years, Kamen has been working on projects to make people's lives better. He says, "I don't work on a project unless I believe that it will dramatically improve life for a bunch of people."

How did Kamen come up with the idea for the IBOT™? Years ago, he noticed a young man in the street unsuccessfully trying to get his wheelchair onto a curb. Kamen started thinking about how to improve the wheelchair. Then, one day, while he was stepping out of the shower, he slipped. To regain his balance, he swiveled around quickly. This action led Kamen to develop the self-balancing technology of the IBOT™, which uses sensors and microprocessors to keep its balance.

Kamen has been keeping his invention secret for some time, but now the news is out, and the device will become available in the not-too-distant future.

Grammar focus

1 **Look at the examples. Which ones are the present perfect and which are the present perfect continuous? Label the sentences *pp* or *ppc*.**

Dean Kamen **has come up with** a design for a revolutionary new wheelchair.
He **has been working on** projects to make people's lives better.
Trevor Baylis **has won** several prizes for his work.
He**'s been developing** a power device that creates electricity as people walk.

2 **Look at the examples again. Complete the rules in the chart with *present perfect* or *present perfect continuous*.**

Present perfect and present perfect continuous
Use the __________ to talk about past achievements. It focuses on the result of a completed action.
Use the __________ to talk about an activity that began in the past and may continue up to the present. It focuses on the continuation of an action.
To form the __________, use *have/has* + the past participle.
To form the __________, use *have/has* + *been* + *verb* + *-ing*.

Grammar Reference page 143

3 **Underline the correct phrase to complete each sentence.**

1. They have **built / been building** a new boat for the past year. It should be ready soon.
2. I haven't **studied / been studying** for my exam yet, and now it's too late.
3. Joanna has **won / been winning** three prizes for her paintings.
4. I've **passed / been passing** all my exams, and now I'm taking a vacation!
5. They're exhausted because they've **prepared / been preparing** for next week's sales meeting.
6. Mike has **received / been receiving** his certificate in teaching.
7. At last, she's **finished / been finishing** her chemistry project.
8. I've **read / been reading** this fascinating book about inventors. I can lend it to you when I'm done.

Pronunciation

4 **Listen. Notice the pronunciation of the weak and contracted forms of *have* and *has*.**

Trevor has won several prizes.
What else has he invented?
What have you been working on?
He's developed many windup devices.
He's been working on a device that creates electricity.
I've been developing a new computer game.

5 **Listen again and repeat.**

Speaking

6 *BEFORE YOU SPEAK.* **Write three things that you have achieved in your life and three recent ongoing activities.**

Achievements	Ongoing activities
I've received an important award at work.	I've been taking karate lessons.

7 *PAIRS.* **Talk about your achievements and ongoing activities. Ask each other follow-up questions.**

A: Barbara, tell me about something you've achieved.
B: I've received an important award at work.
A: What was it for?

8 **Tell the class about your partner's achievements and ongoing activities.**

Writing

9 **Write a brief application letter for one of the following. Include a description of your achievements and any ongoing activities.**

- an advertised job you're interested in
- a club you would like to join
- a college or university you would like to attend

CONVERSATION TO GO

A: What **have you been doing** lately?
B: I**'ve been developing** a new computer game. It's really cool!

Corporate spying

Vocabulary Crime
Grammar Expressions of purpose: *to, in order to, so that, for, in case*
Speaking Describing reasons for doing things

Lesson A

Getting started

1 **Underline the correct words to complete the sentences.**

1. The security guard spent the night **looking at / spying on** the closed circuit TVs.
2. The director **committed / was accused of** using company profits to buy a new home. He claimed he was innocent.
3. Detectives often try to **uncover / protect** people's illegal activities.
4. An employee was **suspected of / convicted of** stealing property, but it was impossible to prove.
5. When you apply for a credit card, the financial institution **restricts / checks on** your personal finances.
6. Would you please **keep an eye on / keep tabs on** my bike while I get coffee?
7. Dishonest people try to **take advantage of / get away with** cheating innocent victims.
8. Security cameras are believed to **deter / eavesdrop on** criminals.

2 *PAIRS.* **Make sentences with an appropriate form of the words you did not underline in Exercise 1.**

The police spied on the suspect for months before they arrested him.

3 *PAIRS.* **Do you think it is OK for employees to do these things at work?**

- take pens home
- send personal emails
- make personal phone calls
- claim more money on their expense accounts than they have really spent

Listening

4 **A business executive is meeting with a sales representative from a security firm. Listen to their conversation and check (✓) the picture(s) of the item or items that the executive might be interested in buying.**

5 *GROUPS OF 4.* **What is your opinion of corporate spying? Do companies have a right to spy on their workers? What rights do employees have?**

A: I think companies have to watch their workers closely in order to protect their property.
B: I think employees have a greater right to privacy.

Reading

6 **Look at the photo in the magazine article. What are the security guards doing? What do you think they are looking for?**

7 **Read the article quickly and match the headings with the correct paragraphs.**

They Know Where You Are!

Do You Take Office Pens?

Your Computer Can't Hide.

Someone's Watching You!

1. ____________________

Admit it! Sometimes you make a few personal phone calls at work. You take home some office pens. You come back a little late after lunch. You always thought nobody noticed. No one could accuse you of stealing! But not any more! From now on, employers will be taking advantage of new technology in order to spy on employees. And that means you!

2. ____________________

You may not see them, but tiny tape recorders and video cameras are probably spying on you now. They are security devices for watching and listening to everything that happens at the workplace. And don't try to hide! They can even check on workers to see if they are really where they say they are. Companies can link cameras to offices in case workers are tempted to steal property. They can install machines in sales representatives' cars to check on their expense accounts.

3. ____________________

And what's more, businesses are bringing in security companies to watch employees' virtual movements. Software is installed so that they can record the websites you visit and check the emails you send. They uncover all your secrets. You have been warned!

8 **Read the article again. Write *T* (true) or *F* (false) next to each statement.**

1. Companies install video cameras and tape recorders in the workplace to check that employees aren't doing anything illegal. T
2. Employers put machines in their employees' cars in order to prevent the cars from being stolen. F
3. "Virtual movements" in paragraph 3 refers to things people do with their computers, such as visiting websites. T
4. Computer software allows employers to keep an eye on their employees' email. T

Grammar focus

1 **Study the examples of expressions of purpose. Notice the ways to express reasons.**

Companies use surveillance	**to** watch employees' virtual movements. **in order to** spy on employees. **so that** they can record the websites workers visit. **in case** workers are tempted to steal property. **for** watching and listening to everything.

2 **Look at the examples again. Complete the rules in the chart with *verb*, *verb + -ing*, or *subject + verb*.**

Expressions of purpose	
Why someone does something:	**Because something might happen:**
to + <u>verb</u>	*in case* + ______
in order to + ______	**What something is for:**
so that + ______	*for* + ______

Grammar Reference page 143

3 **Use *to, in order to, so that, in case,* and *for*. Combine the beginnings of the sentences on the left with the endings on the right to make logical sentences.**

Some companies use microphones and video cameras to find evidence of dishonest employees.

1. Some companies use microphones and video cameras
2. Cell phones are very useful
3. Before you start a trip, you should leave all your contact information with a relative
4. Security cameras are used in stores
5. Many people use identification devices in their phones
6. Some companies use software
7. Some parents install hidden video cameras at home
8. The police sometimes use hidden microphones

a. there is an emergency.
b. catching shoplifters.
c. watching the babysitter while they're out.
d. they can ignore unwanted calls.
e. they can check on employees' computer use.
f. find evidence of dishonest employees.
g. eavesdrop on criminals.
h. staying in contact with teenagers while they're out with friends.

Pronunciation

4 *PAIRS.* **One word in each line does not have the stress shown by the pattern of big and small circles. Underline the word that has a different stress pattern.**

O o	problems, cameras, suspect (noun), protect, software
o O	deter, office, suspect (verb), accused, install
O o o	company, evidence, monitor, criminal, surveillance
o O o	property, solutions, employees, advantage, devices
o O o o	security, technology, information, responsible

5 **Listen and check your answers. Notice the stress in the words.**

6 **Listen again and repeat.**

Speaking

7 *PAIRS.* **Imagine you have the following jobs. You and your partner are going to have a meeting about company security.**

Student A, look at page 137. Student B, look at page 141.

A: Our employees may be making long personal calls because our phone bill went up by 30 percent. Can you help me with this problem?
B: Yes, we can. We have something called "Call Stopper," which many companies use to stop long phone calls.
A: How much does it cost?

8 **Report to the class what you and your partner agreed on and the reasons for the decision.**

Writing

9 **You are the president of a company. Write an email to your employees. Explain some new security devices that you are going to start using or stop using. Explain the reason for your decision.**

Conversation to Go

A: Why are you putting in security cameras?
B: So that I'll know where I am.

UNIT 8

Up in the air

Vocabulary Travel and airports
Grammar Past perfect
Speaking Talking about events in your life

Lesson **A**

Getting started

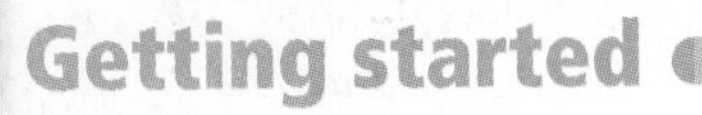

1 *PAIRS.* **Look at the pictures of people, places, and things related to air travel. Write the letters of the pictures next to the correct words.**

baggage claim _G_	luggage ____
boarding pass ____	flight attendant ____
carry-on bag ____	gate ____
check-in counter ____	runway ____
duty-free shops ____	security checkpoint ____

2 *PAIRS.* **Take turns asking each other these questions. Explain what happened and ask and answer follow-up questions.**

Have you ever . . .
- missed a flight?
- lost your luggage?
- gone to the wrong gate?
- been stopped at a security checkpoint?
- had any other problems while traveling?

Reading

3 **Read the article quickly. Did the traveler have a positive or negative experience at the airport?**

LOSING YOURSELF AT THE AIRPORT

The Hub

Sometimes you fly, not to your destination, but to a "hub." In other words, you have to change planes at some airport you never cared to be in. You sit in the airport lounge where all the seats face the same direction, like the seats in a theater, with nothing to do but kill time.

You drift off to sleep. When you wake up, you don't know what time it is. In many airports, each terminal is the same as every other terminal. The corridors are also all the same. But gate 36 may be hundreds of meters from gate 35, in any direction—it's easy to make a mistake.

I was once at an airport in Zurich. The weather was bad and the plane was delayed. I went to a café. I sat there drinking coffee and reading a book. Outside, the weather had gotten worse. Time passed. When the flight was announced, I picked up my bags and moved toward the gate. I went down a corridor, down some steps, straight for a bit, down for a bit. Then, just as I got to the gate, I realized I had left my book in the café.

I tried to remember the route I had taken so I could do it in reverse. I was successful. The book was still there. Then I started running back. I ran up staircases, along corridors. At some point, I knew that I had taken the wrong turn. I panicked.

Adapted from *The Observer* newspaper

4 **Read the article again. Write *T* (true) or *F* (false) after each statement.**

1. You land at a hub to catch another plane.
2. It is easy to go to the wrong gate.
3. When the author went back, he couldn't find the book.
4. The author got lost in the airport.

Listening

5 **Listen to two people talking at an airport while they wait for their plane. What happened to Lou? Number the events in the correct order.**

1 He got delayed in traffic.	5 The plane returned to the gate.
6 He boarded the plane.	2 He was late for his flight.
3 The plane left the gate.	4 He went to the gate.

6 *PAIRS.* **Was Lou right to do what he did? Would you do the same thing?**

Grammar focus

1 **Study the example of the past perfect. Notice the timeline.**

By the time he reached the gate, his plane **had** already **left**.

2 **Look at the examples again. Underline the correct information to complete the rules in the chart.**

Past perfect
Use the past perfect to talk about an action that happened **before / after** another action in the past.
Form the past perfect with *had* + the **infinitive / past participle**.
When you use *already* with the past perfect, it goes **before / after** *had*.
Use the **simple past / past perfect** tense in clauses that begin with *by the time*.
NOTE: You can use contractions with subject pronouns and ***had***; for example, ***He'd gotten stuck***.

Grammar Reference page 144

3 **Complete the sentences using the correct form of the past perfect or the simple past of the verbs in parentheses.**

1. He got (**get**) to the airport late because he had gotten stuck (**get stuck**) in traffic.
2. When we got to the beach, we ____________ (**want**) to go swimming, but we realized that we ____________ (**not/pack**) our swimsuits.
3. We ____________ (**have**) a wonderful time on our skiing vacation. The kids ____________ (**never/see**) snow before.
4. As soon as I saw Jong-Mi, I ____________ (**realize**) I ____________ (**meet**) her before.
5. I knew I ____________ (**not/study**) enough as soon as I ____________ (**see**) the first exam question.
6. I ____________ (**not/laugh**) at the joke because I ____________ (**hear**) it so many times before.
7. When she ____________ (**ask**) to see my boarding pass, I realized I ____________ (**lose**) it.
8. I ____________ (**not/call**) you this morning because I thought you ____________ (**already/go out**).

Pronunciation

4 **Listen. Notice the pronunciation of the weak and contracted forms of *had*.**

I'd forgotten my book.

He'd already checked out of the hotel.

His plane had already left the gate.

I realized I had left it in the café.

He was late because he'd gotten stuck in traffic.

But it **hadn't** taken off yet.

5 **Listen again and repeat.**

Speaking

6 BEFORE YOU SPEAK. **Think of something interesting or important that happened to you. It could be about travel, your family, your job, or something else.**

- Decide on six key words or events in the story.
- Write them in the boxes in the order they happened.

7 PAIRS. **Tell the story of your experience. Start at number four (in the past). For things that happened before then, use the past perfect.**

I missed a plane. I'd been on vacation and had already checked out of the hotel. I was late because I'd gotten stuck in traffic on the way to the airport.

Writing

8 **Write a story of an interesting experience that happened to you or to someone you know. Use the past perfect tense.**

Conversation to go

A: Did you say good-bye to her at the airport?
B: No. By the time I arrived, her flight had already left.

Review 2

Units 5–8

Unit 5 How rude!

1 *PAIRS.* Role-play the following situations. Take turns asking for and giving/denying permission.

1. Your neighbor has no hot water in her home. She knocks at your door and asks you if she can use your bathroom.
2. You are sitting at an outdoor café when a man at the next table wants to smoke. You can't stand smoke anywhere near you.
3. A friend who is staying with you wants to use your phone to call his or her brother in England.
4. You are the boss at work. Someone who works for you needs to leave early today. This person has arrived late every day this week.
5. You are in a waiting room in a doctor's office with a few other people. There's a TV that's not turned on. Another person wants to turn on the TV.

2 Create two new situations and role-play them.

Unit 6 Achievement

3 Listen to a description of an achievement by an inventor. Answer these questions.

1. What has Mohammed Bah Abba invented?
2. What does his invention do?
3. What has he been trying to do since he came up with his idea?

4 *GROUPS OF 3.* Can you think of any inventions or achievements that have changed the way we live, in small or big ways? Describe them and explain how they have made a difference.

Mohammed Bah Abba

Unit 7 Corporate spying

5 Read the article about camera phones. What are the arguments for and against their use?

In the Public Eye

One evening last month, grocery store owner Sam Lee was about to close his shop when a man came in, waving a knife at Sam and demanding money. Instead of giving him money, Sam pulled out his cell phone and used it to snap a picture of the robber. The man ran off, but within minutes, Sam had transmitted the picture to his computer. When police arrived, Sam had the man's picture waiting for them.

Camera phones may be used for spying on people who don't suspect it. For example, police could use camera phones in order to identify criminals or missing persons, but they could also use them to photograph protestors. Some fitness centers have banned camera phones so that they can keep spying eyes out of locker rooms. Businesses are already looking into ways of using camera phones in order to check on employees' whereabouts. Critics worry that these phones may change our way of life, and not for the better.

6 *PAIRS.* Have a debate for and against the use of camera phones. Give examples of what people will use them for.

Unit 8 Up in the air

7 *PAIRS.* Listen to a conversation between two friends. Complete the story with your own ideas.

8 *PAIRS.* Take turns telling stories of interesting travel experiences that happened to you or someone you know. Give the background details of what had happened earlier.

UNIT 9

Sunshine and showers

Vocabulary The weather
Grammar Indirect statements
Speaking Reporting what you hear or read

Lesson A

B

A

C

Getting started

1 **Complete the sentences with the words in the box. There may be more than one answer.**

~~cloud cover~~	clouds	fog	rain
showers	snow	sunshine	thunderstorms
tornado	winds		

1. It isn't raining today, but there is a very thick _cloud cover_.
2. There was heavy _rain_ during the night and some roads were flooded.
3. You probably won't need an umbrella—there will be just light _showers_ today.
4. A tree was hit by lightning during severe _thunderstorms_ yesterday.
5. During the summer in Greece, there is bright _sunshine_ every day.
6. _Snow_ will fall tonight, especially in the mountains.
7. There were very strong _winds_, and several trees were blown down.
8. It was difficult to see while I was driving because of the dense _fog_.
9. A deadly _tornado_ carved its path across the region.
10. Look at those dark _clouds_! It's going to rain any minute.

2 *PAIRS.* **Discuss these questions.**

What kind of weather is typical of different parts of your country?
Are there any sayings (or proverbs) about the weather in your country?

Listening

3 **Listen to a meteorologist discuss different kinds of extreme events of nature. Then label the pictures with the words in the box.**

hurricane / typhoon	tornado	tsunami

Reading

4 *PAIRS.* **Look at the photo in the newspaper article. What do you think happened?**

5 **Read the newspaper article and answer these questions.**

1. When do tornados often happen?
2. What was the main cause of this unusual tornado?
3. What were three results of the tornado?
4. What other word for *tornado* can you find in the article?

6 *PAIRS.* **Discuss. What extreme events from nature do you fear most? Why?**

November 13 *The Times*

A Twist of Fate

Deadly Tornado Hits Small Town

Birch Grove, November 13 — It was nice and calm at noon yesterday, though unusually hot for November. In the evening, dark clouds appeared, then lightning and rain started, and then came the wind. Suddenly, a devastating tornado swept across the region, leaving at least five people dead and others missing.

Speaking at a press conference late last night, the Governor said that thousands of people in neighboring towns were without electricity, but that the lights would be back on by tonight.

The twister left a deadly path behind it. Meteorologist Mark Chaves, describing the devastation, said, "I saw mobile homes thrown into ponds and entire forests wiped out." Tornadoes are common in the spring, rare in the fall. But Chaves said that unseasonably warm weather had made all the difference.

The Farkas family surveys the damage to their home.

Harry Coleman, a resident from the area, was out of town when he got a call from his wife on his cell phone. She told him that their son and grandson were missing. Other residents were luckier. John and Rebecca Reilly's home lost electricity in the rainstorm, but no one was harmed.

Police officer Al Barton said, "I heard a roar and saw the lightning just before the twister came. Then I watched the twister pick up houses and cars, and toss them like toys." Police and rescue crews are still searching for the missing, but dense fog is making their job all the more difficult.

Only a few houses in Birch Grove have basements, and Susan Farkas and her family took shelter in theirs. Within minutes, the house above them began to peel away. Daughter Ginny said, "We all held on to each other and somehow we survived." As the Farkases looked over their broken furniture lying on the ground, Susan told her daughter, "I can't believe it. Yesterday we had a nice house, and today we don't even have a toothbrush."

Grammar focus

1 **Study the examples. Notice the differences between direct and indirect statements.**

Direct statements	Indirect statements
"Our son and grandson are missing."	She **told him (that) their** son and grandson **were** missing.
"I can't believe it."	Susan **said (that)** she **couldn't** believe it.
"The lights will be on by tomorrow night."	Last night the governor **said (that)** the lights **would be** on by **tonight**.
"Unseasonably warm weather made all the difference."	Chaves **said (that)** unseasonably warm weather **had made** all the difference.

2 **Look at the examples again. Complete the rules in the chart with *change* or *don't change*.**

Indirect statements
When changing from direct statements to indirect statements using *said* or *told* + object: The tenses usually ___________. The time expressions usually ___________. The possessive adjectives and pronouns usually ___________.
NOTE: The word *that* is optional after *say* or *tell*.

Grammar Reference page 144

3 **Rewrite the sentences in indirect speech. Make any necessary changes.**

1. He said, "Thousands of people are still without electricity."
   He said that thousands of people were still without electricity.
2. They said, "It is one of the worst tornadoes in years."
3. He said, "I saw mobile homes thrown into ponds."
4. Susan told her daughter, "We don't even have a toothbrush."
5. He said, "I heard a roar and saw the lightning."
6. She told me, "Somehow we survived."
7. The Governor said, "The government will do everything it can to assist families."
8. Last night the meteorologist said, "It's unlikely there will be any more tornadoes tonight."

Pronunciation

4 **Listen. Notice the pronunciation of the voiceless *th* sound /θ/ in the words in the first row and the voiced *th* sound /ð/ in the words in the second row.**

thunderstorm	**th**ousands	every**th**ing	**th**rown	pa**th**
they	**th**ere	wi**th**out	o**th**er	**th**e wea**th**er

What did **th**ey say about **th**e wea**th**er? **Th**ey said **th**ere would be **th**ick clouds and **th**understorms.

5 **Listen again and repeat.**

Speaking

6 *GROUPS OF 3.* **You've made plans to have a beach party tomorrow. You're each getting the weather forecast from a different TV channel. Based on the weather forecasts, decide together if you are still going to the beach.**

Student A, look at page 137. Student B, look at page 138. Student C, look at page 140.

On Channel 12 they said that there was a storm coming from the south. It will probably rain at times.

7 **Look at page 141 to check the actual weather on the day of the beach party. Was your decision correct?**

Writing

8 **Write an email to a friend who is planning to visit you tomorrow. Tell your friend how the weather is today and what you think it will be like tomorrow.**

CONVERSATION TO GO

A: Have you heard the weather report?
B: Yes. They said there would be heavy rain all day.

Tomorrow's world

Vocabulary Describing changes
Grammar Simple future and future perfect
Speaking Predicting future events

Lesson **A**

Getting started

1 *PAIRS.* **Look at the pairs of words. Underline the three additional pairs that describe up/down changes.**

go up / go down	decrease / increase	fall / rise
improve / deteriorate	climb / drop	get better / get worse

2 *PAIRS.* **Look at the list of topics. Make predictions about them. Use the words from Exercise 1 in your predictions.**

I think pollution will start to decrease.

- pollution
- crime
- health care
- life expectancy
- quality of life
- education

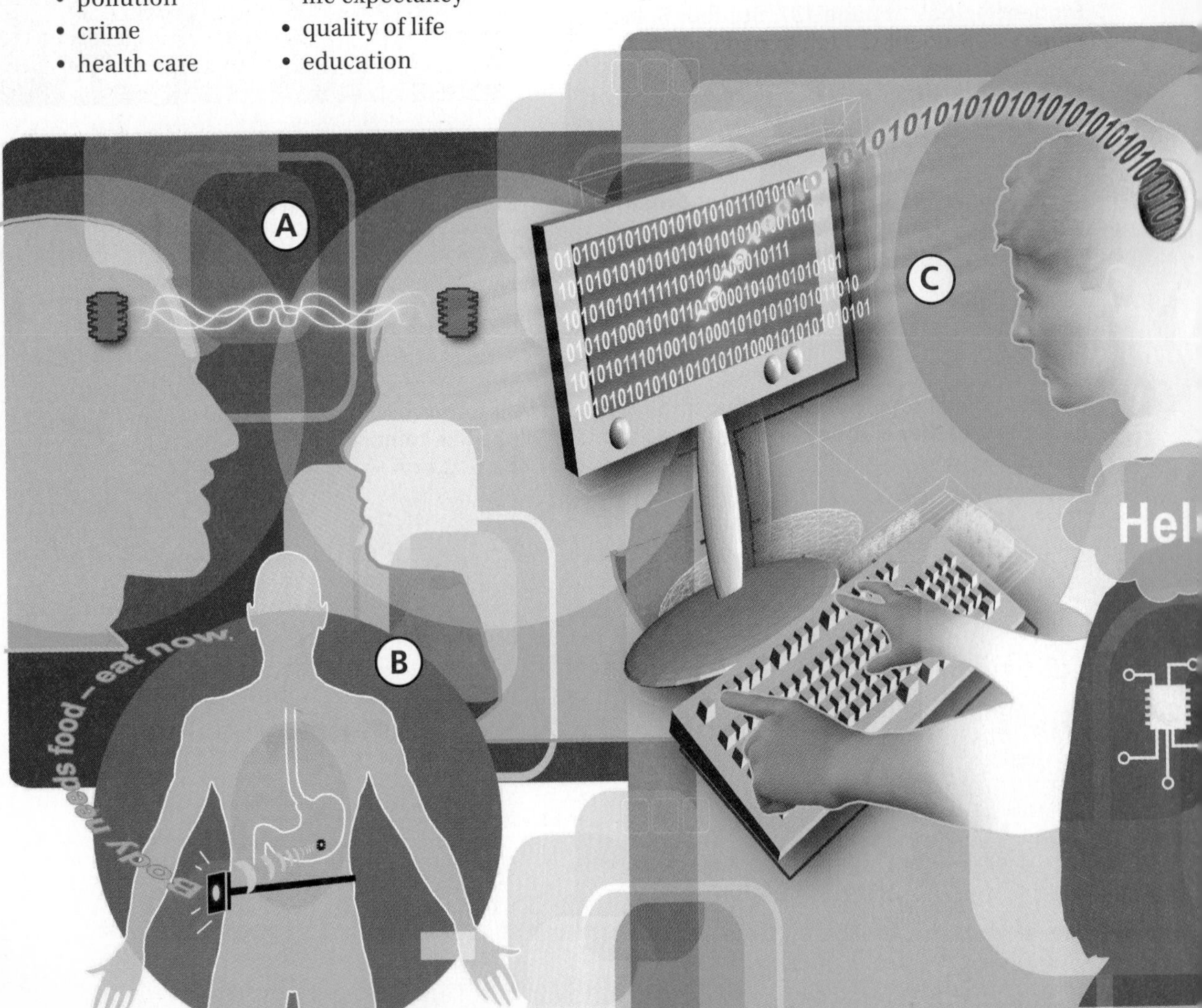

Reading

3 **Look at the pictures of future technological advances and describe what you think is happening in each.**

It looks like computers inside the people's brains are communicating with each other.

4 **Read the magazine article about predictions for technological advances. Write the letter of each picture next to the paragraph that describes it.**

What Will the Future Look Like?

A bright future or Frankenstein's monster?

___ By 2075, scientists will have produced edible computers—you can eat one per day. They will record everything that's going on inside you and carry this information to a small box that you wear on your belt. These systems will be invaluable to doctors and will dramatically improve health care.

___ Methods of communication are advancing—by the year 2150, scientists will have perfected the "brainlink" computer. A tiny computer will be implanted under the skin on the back of people's heads, which will tell their brains how to speak any language they need. Just imagine! People will be able to go to another country and order a meal in a restaurant without using a dictionary!

___ Computers could be connected to people's brains by the end of the 22nd century. As a result, the number of schools will decrease, or they may even disappear completely. People will simply be able to download information into their heads. Imagine being able to store all the knowledge you need in your brain without memorizing!

___ By the 23rd century, scientists will have developed a technique for implanting computer chips in people's brains. People will be able to communicate by simply using their brainwaves. But will they want to?

5 **Read the article again. What do you think will be the benefit of each technological advance?**

- edible computers
- "brainlink" computers
- computers connected to brains
- implanted computer chips

Listening

6 **Listen to the radio interview with Dr. Pierce. Write a plus sign (+) next to the technological advances in Exercise 5 that she thinks are positive, and a minus sign (–) next to the ones she thinks are negative.**

7 *PAIRS.* **Discuss these questions.**

Do you think these advances will actually happen?

If they do, do you think they will improve or worsen people's lives? Why?

Grammar focus

1 **Study the examples. Notice the difference between the sentences in the simple future and those in the future perfect tense.**

Simple future	Future perfect
We'**ll be** able to swallow tiny computers.	By the year 2150, scientists **will have perfected** the "brainlink" computer.
They'**ll record** everything that's going on.	By 2075, they'**ll have produced** edible computers.

2 **Look at the examples again. Underline the correct words to complete the rules in the chart.**

Simple future and future perfect
Form the simple future with ***will / will have*** + the base form of the verb.
Form the future perfect with ***will / will have*** + past participle.
Use the simple future when you expect something to happen **at / before** some point in the future.
Use the future perfect when you expect something to happen **at / before** some point in the future.

Grammar Reference page 144

3 **Use the cues to complete the sentences. Use only one word in each blank.**

1. Life expectancy will have ___increased___ **(increase)** to over 100 by 2070.
2. Someday all cars will __________________ **(use)** energy from the sun instead of gas.
3. In the next five years, communication will __________________ **(become)** much quicker.
4. Within 50 years, they will have __________________ **(invent)** cars that reach a destination by themselves.
5. In the next 100 years there will __________________ **(be)** cures for every known disease.
6. By the end of this century, they will have __________________ **(build)** underground cities in many countries around the world.
7. Someday blind people will __________________ **(have)** robots to guide them.
8. By 2025, keys will have __________________ **(disappear)**. Instead, special sensors will __________________ **(identify)** people and open doors for them.

4 *PAIRS.* **Which predictions in Exercise 3 do you agree with? Explain.**

Pronunciation

5 **Listen. Notice the pronunciation of the contracted and weak forms of *will* and the way *will* is linked to the weak form of *have*.**

We'll be able to swallow tiny computers.

Communication will be easier.

We'll have learned to communicate by brainwaves.

They'll record what's going on.

Scientists will have perfected the brainlink computer.

They'll have found ways to read people's thoughts.

6 **Listen again and repeat.**

Speaking

7 *BEFORE YOU SPEAK.* **Think about your future. Where will you be and what will you have accomplished? Think about at least three ideas related to things like education, career, family, sports, hobbies and travel. Take notes.**

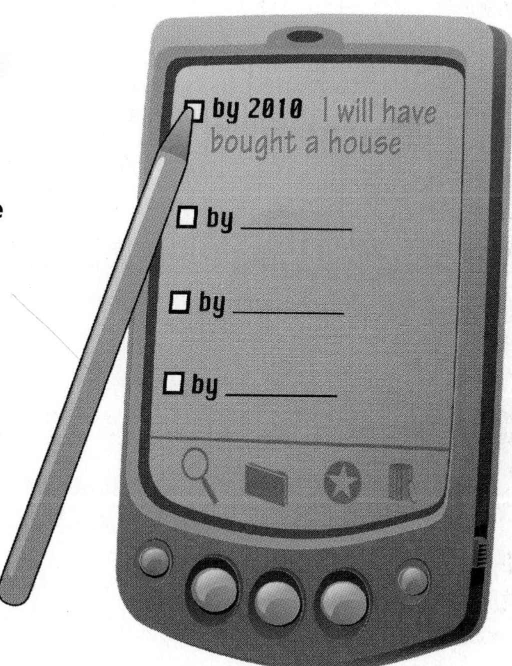

8 *PAIRS.* **Take turns talking about your predictions for the future.**

I predict that by the year 2010,
I will have bought a house.

9 **Report to the class. What were at least two predictions your partner made?**

Writing

10 **Write a diary entry about things you believe you will have done five years from now. Write about career, marriage, family, travel, or any other things you can imagine will have happened.**

CONVERSATION TO GO

A: When will you be finished with your homework? Dinner will be ready in about an hour.
B: I'll probably have finished it by breakfast time tomorrow!

How did it go?

Vocabulary Job interviews
Grammar Indirect questions
Speaking Reporting a conversation or interview

Lesson A

Getting started

1 *PAIRS.* **Discuss these questions.**

Which kinds of interviews have you been on?

How do you feel before, during, and after an interview?

2 *PAIRS.* **Look at the "Top Tips for Job Interviews" and underline the correct word or phrase in each tip.**

Top Tips for Job Interviews

1. Make a list of your **strengths / prospects.** It's important to talk about what you are good at.
2. Make a list of your **qualifications / weaknesses**. Interviewers sometimes ask what you are *not* good at.
3. Prepare to talk about your past **experience / promotion.** You can talk about things you have done that relate to this job.
4. Make sure you know which relevant **qualifications / long-term goals** you have. Certificates, diplomas, and degrees are important.
5. Think of two past employers who will write good **prospects / references** for you. The interviewer will need to know what past employers thought of your work.
6. Show that you are interested in **experience / promotion.** It's impressive to show interest in getting better jobs in the company in the future.
7. Be clear about your **long-term goals / qualifications**. Interviewers sometimes ask what your five-year plan is.
8. Be realistic about your job **references / prospects**. Don't waste your time applying for a job if you know you are unqualified.

Reading

3 *PAIRS.* **Read the list of tips in Exercise 2 again. Match each of these statements with the correct tip.**

1. "I have a degree in communications."
2. "I think I work well under pressure, and I'm well organized."
3. "I used to work at a bank. My former supervisor would be glad to recommend me."
4. "Because I like to work fast, I sometimes do things in a bit of a hurry."
5. "I'd like to move from sales to management someday."
6. "I was treasurer of my school's computer club, so I'm used to handling money."

4 *GROUPS OF 3.* **Discuss the following as they apply to your school or work life.**

My main strength is creativity, I think. I find it fun to work with new ideas.

- your main strengths
- your qualifications
- your long-term goals

Listening

5 **Listen to Carol telling a friend about her job interview. Check (✓) the topics discussed in the interview.**

- ☐ previous experience
- ☐ working under pressure
- ☐ strengths
- ☐ long-term goals
- ☐ weaknesses
- ☐ reasons for leaving previous jobs
- ☐ salary
- ☐ taking breaks during work

6 **Listen again and answer these questions.**

1. How does Carol think the interview went?
2. What did she ask the interviewer about?
3. Did the interview go better or worse than Carol thought? How do you know?

Grammar focus

1 **Study the examples. Notice the differences between direct and indirect questions.**

Direct questions	Indirect questions
A. "What are your strengths?"	She asked me **what my strengths were**.
B. "Do you have other weaknesses?"	She wanted me to tell her **if I had other weaknesses**.
C. "Can you work under pressure?"	She wanted to know **whether I could work under pressure**.

2 **Look at the examples again. Underline the correct words to complete the rules in the chart.**

Indirect questions
The verb tense in direct and indirect questions is often the **same / different**.
For indirect questions that ask for information (example A), use **a *Wh-* word / *if***.
For indirect *Yes/No* questions (examples B and C), use **a *Wh-* word / *if***.
In indirect questions, use **subject + verb / verb + subject** after the *Wh-* word or *if*.
NOTE: With indirect questions, *if* and *whether* mean the same thing.

Grammar Reference page 144

3 **Change the direct questions to indirect questions. Use different ways of starting indirect questions.**

He wanted to know what the responsibilities of the job were. OR
He asked her what the responsibilities of the job were.

Pronunciation

4 🎧 **Listen. Notice the groups of consonant sounds in these words.**

pressure	**pr**omotion	**pr**o**sp**e**cts**	e**xp**erie**nc**e
stay	**st**art	**str**e**ngths**	a**sked**

She a**sked** about my **pr**evious e**xp**erie**nc**e.

I to**ld** her I work well under **pr**essure.

She a**sked** me how long I **planned** to **st**ay.

She a**sked** me what my **str**e**ngths** were.

I a**sked** her about the **pr**o**sp**e**cts** for **pr**omotion.

She a**sked** me when I could **st**art.

5 🎧 **Listen again and repeat.**

Speaking

6 *BEFORE YOU SPEAK.* **Think about a situation when someone asked you questions. The situation might be a job interview, a first date, a visit to the doctor, etc. Complete the chart.**

The situation	
What they asked you	
What you asked them	
How you felt	

7 *PAIRS.* **Take turns describing the situation.**

I had an interview for a part-time job when I was in high school. They asked me why I was interested . . .

Writing

8 **Write a letter to a friend describing an interview or a conversation with someone who asked you questions. Explain the situation, and then report the questions and the answers.**

CONVERSATION TO GO

A: How did it go?

B: Great! He **asked me if I wanted** the job.

Coincidences

Vocabulary Time adverbials
Grammar Narrative past tenses: simple past, past continuous, past perfect, past perfect continuous
Speaking Telling stories in the past

Lesson A

Getting started

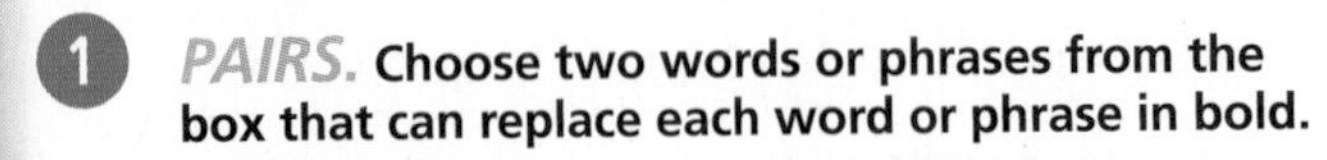

1 *PAIRS.* **Choose two words or phrases from the box that can replace each word or phrase in bold.**

~~afterward~~	at the same time
earlier	every time
previously	simultaneously
~~subsequently~~	whenever

1. Have you ever been introduced to someone but forgotten their name **later**?
   afterward / subsequently
2. Are there any places that remind you of someone **each time** you go there?
   ______ / ______
3. Have you ever experienced something that you had dreamed about **before**?
   ______ / ______
4. Have you and another person ever said exactly the same thing **at the same moment**?
   ______ / ______

2 *PAIRS.* **Take turns asking and answering the questions in Exercise 1.**

Reading

3 **Look at the pictures in the article. What do you think is happening in each?**

4 **Read about some real-life coincidences. Then match the titles with the stories.**

Family Reunion | **The Wrong Number**

A Shared History | **Life Saver**

5 **Read the article again. Explain in your own words what each coincidence was.**

6 *PAIRS.* **Discuss these questions.**

Which coincidence do you find most amazing?
Which would you describe as a lucky coincidence? A strange coincidence?

You'll Never Believe It!

1.

John Peskett—who first met his wife, Shirley, when he was 21—discovered, when she showed him her favorite childhood photo, that he and his family had been sitting next to her on the same beach twenty years earlier.

2.

A young man, Harold Archer, threw himself in front of a train, but was saved—an inch from death—by a passenger on the train who had pulled the emergency cord without knowing about Archer. The passenger said afterward that she had pulled the cord because she "suddenly felt she should."

3.

Charlie Crook one day decided to drive over 100 miles (160 km) to visit his cousin, John Barker, whom he hadn't seen for eight years. Barker had simultaneously decided to drive and see Charlie—and met him halfway, where their cars collided.

4.

Police officer Peter Moscardi, on night patrol, became suspicious when he saw an open door in a factory. He entered the factory office and decided to pick up a phone that was ringing. It was a friend of his calling to chat. Moscardi had previously given his friend the police station phone's last four numbers incorrectly—that number was the factory's telephone number.

Adapted from ES Magazine

Listening

7 **Listen to a man tell the story of an event that happened to him. Answer these questions.**

1. What was the coincidence?
2. How do you think the man felt when he realized what had happened?

Grammar focus

1 **Study the examples of narrative past tenses. Notice how different tenses are used.**

A passenger on the train **pulled** the emergency cord.

He **decided** to pick up a phone that **was ringing**.

He **discovered** that he and his family **had been sitting** next to her on the same beach twenty years earlier.

Charlie Crook **decided** to visit his cousin, John Barker, whom he **hadn't seen** for eight years.

2 **Look at the examples again. Complete the rules in the chart with *simple past, past continuous, past perfect,* or *past perfect continuous.***

Narrative past tenses: simple past, past continuous, past perfect, past perfect continuous
______________ refers to an action that was in progress when something else happened.
______________ refers to a completed action in the past.
______________ refers to an action completed before another event or time in the past.
______________ refers to an action that was in progress before another event or time in the past.

Grammar Reference page 145

3 **Read the story. Then put the verbs into the correct tenses.**

Irene Jones and Stella Frank, both from Texas, grew up (1. grow up) on the same street and ______ (2. become) best friends. Stella was Irene's bridesmaid at her wedding. Then Irene moved away, and they ______ (3. lose) touch. Fifty-three years later, they ______ (4. bump) into each other while they ______ (5. wait) in line at a gas station in Boulder, Colorado. They immediately ______ (6. recognize) each other, even though they ______ (7. not see) each other for over fifty years. While they ______ (8. talk), they ______ (9. find out) they ______ (10. live) in the same neighborhood in Boulder for 17 years, but ______ (11. never see) each other until that day.

Pronunciation

4 **Listen to the beginning of the story in Exercise 3. Notice that only the important words are stressed.**

Irene Jones and **Stel**la **Frank**, **both** from **Tex**as, grew **up** on the **same street**.

5 **Listen to more of the story. Underline the stressed words on page 54.**

Speaking

6 *BEFORE YOU SPEAK.* **What are five important events in your life (for example, you got your first job, you graduated from school, you got married, etc.)? Think about the events that led up to each one. Take notes.**

Date, important event	Background
2000: I graduated from school	I had been studying for four years and . . .

7 *GROUPS OF 4.* **Take turns talking about the special events in your life and the events that led up to them.**

8 **Report to the class. Are there any coincidences or similarities between the events in your group?**

Two years ago, I moved to this area. I had been living in Pleasantville before. It turns out that Marta had once lived in Pleasantville, too.

Writing

9 **Write a story about several important events in your life and the circumstances that led up to them.**

CONVERSATION TO GO

A: What **were** you **doing** at ten o'clock last night, sir?
B: I **was watching** TV. I**'d been** out with my friends in the afternoon.

Units 9–12

Unit 9 Sunshine and showers

1 GROUPS OF 4. Listen to weather forecasts for different cities. Each student listens to the report for one city and takes notes.

Student	City	Today	Tomorrow
A	Tokyo, Japan		
B	Ottawa, Canada		
C	Recife, Brazil		
D	Santiago, Chile		

2 GROUPS OF 4. Take turns reporting on the forecasts you took notes on. What did the meteorologist say about the weather now and for the future? Take notes on your partners' reports.

Unit 10 Tomorrow's world

3 Listen to a conversation between two friends about a movie called *Sleeper*. What is the movie about?

4 Imagine you fall asleep and wake up 200 years in the future. Write down some ideas about what will have happened by the time you wake up, and how life will be different in the 23rd century.

5 PAIRS. Discuss your ideas about the future.

Unit 11 How did it go?

6 Read the ad. You are going to role-play an interview for the job advertised.

> **Salesperson Wanted**
>
> Excellent opportunity to be a salesperson in an electronics superstore. Competitive salary & benefits. Experience in sales and/or electronics is preferred. Work some nights/weekends. Call 555-4321.

7 *PAIRS.* Role-play the job interview.

Student A, look at page 139. Student B, look at page 140.

8 *GROUPS OF 4.* Report the questions and answers from your interview in Exercise 7.

A: I asked him if he had any sales experience.
C: And what did he say?

Unit 12 Coincidences

9 Read the facts in "All in the family" related to the story of three men. What was their relationship? Why was it an amazing coincidence?

10 *PAIRS.* Together, tell the story of Gary and his long-lost brothers. You can start like this:

When Gary's first child was born, his parents told him that he was an adopted child. That conversation changed his life forever.

11 *PAIRS.* Do you know any stories of amazing coincidences? Take turns telling the stories. Include any background information.

All in the family

- Steve and Gary were best friends. In fact, they were like brothers; Gary was best man at Steve's wedding.
- Steve was adopted. He knew this but didn't know his real parents.
- Gary was adopted too, but he didn't know it because his parents never told him.
- Gary had a good friend named Richard who worked out at the same fitness center.
- Richard was also adopted but didn't know who his real parents were.
- After Gary's first child was born, his parents decided to tell him that he was adopted.
- When Gary found out that he was adopted, he got together with Steve and Richard. Pretty soon, they figured out that they were all brothers! They learned later that they were among nine children given up for adoption by a couple who had thirteen children.
- The brothers were shocked, but delighted, to find each other. Gary said it was "the greatest gift in the world."

World of Music 2

Words Get in the Way

Gloria Estefan

Vocabulary

1 *PAIRS.* **Match the clauses on the left with the appropriate information on the right to make logical sentences.**

1. I've been **seeing** _f_
2. I never know what to expect from my best friend because ____
3. It's hard to be with someone who ____
4. When I have **something on my mind,** ____
5. Some people get very nervous if they feel ____
6. When you lose someone you love, ____
7. I don't let my social life ____
8. Animals who were born in captivity often die ____
9. If someone's heart is **an open door,** ____
10. You can still love someone ____

a. I like to talk about it.
b. **despite the fact that** he or she causes you pain.
c. is **temperamental**.
d. it's easy to know how they feel.
e. it **breaks your heart**.
f. someone new.
g. **get in the way** of work or school.
h. if you **set** them **free**.
i. he's totally **moody**. He changes from happy to mad, to happy again five times a day!
j. **locked** inside a small place, such as an elevator.

Gloria Estefan was born in Cuba in 1957. She started her musical career in 1975, when she sang at a wedding where a local band was playing. The band leader, Emilio Estefan, was so impressed by Gloria's voice that he asked her to join his band. Gloria Estefan has enjoyed many successful hits, including "Let it Loose," "Into the Light," and "Gloria!"

Listening

2 **Listen to "Words Get in the Way," by Gloria Estefan. Which statement is true about the singer and her boyfriend? Circle the letter of the correct answer.**

a. She doesn't know how to tell him that she doesn't love him anymore.
b. She's been trying to tell him that he's too temperamental.
c. She has strong feelings but can't express them.

3 **Listen to the song again and complete the lyrics on page 59.**

Words Get in the Way

I realize you're seeing someone new.
I don't believe she knows you like I do;
Your temperamental moody side,
the one you always try to hide from me.

But I know when you have something on your mind.
_____ _____ _____ to tell me for the longest time.
And before you break my heart in two,
There's something _____ _____ _____ to say to you.

But the words get in the way.
There's so much I want to say,
But it's locked deep inside, and if you _____ in
my eyes
We _____ fall in love again.
I won't even start to cry and before we say good-bye.
I tried to say I love you,
But the words got in the way.

Your heart _____ always _____ an open door,
But baby, I don't even know you anymore.
And despite the fact it's hurting me,
I know the time _____ _____ to set you free.

But the words get in the way.
There's so much I want to say,
But it's locked deep inside and if you _____ in
my eyes
We _____ fall in love again.
I won't even start to cry and before we say good-bye.
I tried to say I love you,
But the words got in the way.
I'm trying to say I love you,
But the words get in the way.

Speaking

4 *GROUPS OF 3.* **Discuss these questions. Use lines from the song to explain your answers.**

1. Has the singer's boyfriend told her that he's been dating someone else?
2. What does the singer wish for?
3. What does she want to say to her boyfriend? Why can't she say it?

5 *PAIRS.* **Discuss. Have you ever experienced a time when "the words got in the way"? Explain.**

Going it alone

Vocabulary Adjectives describing fear, loneliness, and nervousness
Grammar Present unreal conditional (*If* + simple past tense form + *would* + verb)
Speaking Talking about hypothetical situations

Lesson **A**

Getting started

1 *PAIRS.* **Look at the adjectives that describe fear, loneliness, and nervousness. Write them next to the words that have similar meanings.**

~~cut off~~	fearful
jumpy	lonesome
solitary	stressed out
isolated	tense
petrified	jittery
scared	terrified

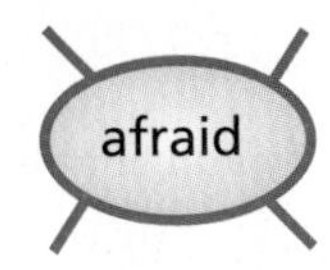

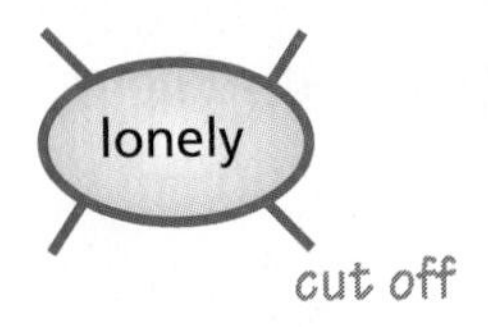

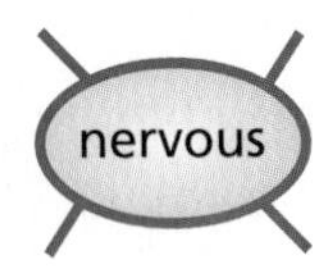

100 days at sea

At the age of 24, Ellen MacArthur became the youngest and the smallest (she is just under 5 feet 2 inches—1.57 meters) competitor to take part in the Vendée Globe race—the biggest challenge in sailing: 100 days alone at sea.

Imagine how it would feel sailing single-handed, nonstop, and unaided around the world, without seeing another person for weeks on end, without knowing when a hurricane could hit your boat and end your chances of finishing or even surviving.

To sail the roughest seas alone, you need great ability and strength —Ellen has both. She remembers everything she reads and hears. "You need so many different skills," Ellen says. "Alone at sea, you are a sailor, an electrician, an engineer, and a cook. There is so much to do so you never feel lonely. I wouldn't do it if I were scared of being alone."

In order to avoid fatigue, Ellen trained to sleep for as little as twenty minutes at a time. "Normal sleep is impossible; you can't sleep for more than four hours a day. If you needed more sleep, you could never finish the race."

During her incredible voyage, she battled against ocean storms, fatigue, and 23 much more experienced competitors, who were mostly men. By the force of her character, Ellen eventually took second place and became a legend.

2 Listen and check your answers.

3 *PAIRS.* **Discuss these questions.**

How do you feel about being . . .
- alone?
- in the dark?
- on an airplane?
- in a very small space?

Reading

4 *PAIRS.* **Look at the photo and discuss these questions.**

Where is this woman?
What is she doing?
How do you think she is feeling?

5 **Read the article to see if your ideas were correct.**

6 **Read the article again. Write *T* (true) or *F* (false) after each statement.**

1. Nobody can help the sailors during the race.
2. Ellen is afraid of being alone.
3. During the race, Ellen had little sleep.
4. Ellen was one of the most experienced competitors in the race.
5. She came in second, so she wasn't very successful.

Listening

7 **Listen to the radio show discussing Ellen MacArthur's life. Answer these questions.**

1. Is Ellen afraid of anything? If so, what?
2. Has she ever finished last in a race? When?
3. Does she think she will win the Jules Verne Challenge? Do *you* think she will?

8 **Listen to the radio broadcast about the Jules Verne Challenge. Were your predictions in Exercise 7 correct?**

Grammar focus

1 **Study the examples of the present unreal conditional. Notice the ways to talk about hypothetical situations.**

> If you **needed** more sleep, you **could** never **finish** the race.
> I **wouldn't** do it if I **were** scared of being alone.

2 **Look at the examples again. Complete the rules in the chart with *the base form of the verb, the simple past form of the verb*, or *would*.**

Present unreal conditional
Form the present unreal conditional with *If* + subject + __________ , subject + *would* or *could* + __________ . If you are less certain, you can use *might* or *could* instead of __________ .
NOTE: Use *were* for all subjects when the verb in the *if* clause is *be*.

Grammar Reference page 145

3 **Rewrite these sentences using the present unreal conditional. Make any necessary changes.**

1. It's too cold. We probably won't go swimming.
   If it weren't so cold, we'd go swimming.
2. I get lonely. I don't want to take part in a solo race.
3. You don't go out a lot. You don't meet many people.
4. I want to call her. I don't know her number.
5. John isn't here. I want to ask him about the weekend.
6. Marta is scared of small spaces. She won't use the elevator.
7. People don't always understand him. He talks too fast.

Pronunciation

4 **Listen to these conditional sentences. Notice the weak and contracted forms of *would* and the weak pronunciation of *could*.**

If it weren't so cold, we'd go swimming.

I wouldn't do it if I were scared of being alone.

If you needed more sleep, you could never finish the race.

5 **Listen again and repeat. Then say the sentences you wrote in Exercise 3. Use contracted or weak forms where possible.**

Speaking

6 *BEFORE YOU SPEAK.* **Imagine being alone for 100 days on a deserted island. What three luxury items would you take with you?**

7 *GROUPS OF 4.* **Tell about the items you would take with you and why. Others in the group will ask questions and fill in the chart.**

A: In Sook, what three items would you take?
B: I'd take a cell phone because . . .

Student's name	Luxury items
In Sook	a cell phone

8 **Report to the class. Say one thing that surprised you about your classmates' answers.**

In Sook would take a cell phone. That surprised me because she wouldn't be able to call anyone from so far away.

Writing

9 **Imagine you are alone—in a solo yacht race, on a deserted island, or in another lonely situation. Imagine it is now day 50 of 100. Write a diary entry about what you would be doing and how you would feel.**

Conversation to Go

A: **If** you **went** to a desert island, what **would** you **take**?
B: **I'd get** very lonely, so I think **I'd take** a friend!

UNIT 14

Commuter blues

Vocabulary Expressions with *time*
Grammar Connectors: *although, despite (not), however, in spite of*
Speaking Comparing attitudes

Lesson A

Getting started

1 *PAIRS.* **Match the beginnings of the sentences on the left with the endings on the right to make logical sentences with expressions with *time*.**

1. He thinks commuting is a **waste** _i_	a. **the time** he gets home.
2. He always arrives at work **on** ____	b. **time for** dinner with his family.
3. He never gets home **in** ____	c. **time off.**
4. He'll have more **leisure** ____	d. **more time** with his family.
5. He always feels stressed **by** ____	e. **of time** until he retires.
6. He would like to **spend** ____	f. **time.**
7. He gets a lot of ____	g. **time** when he retires.
8. His commute **takes** ____	h. **a long time.**
9. It's just **a matter** ____	i. **of time.**

2 *PAIRS.* **Which sentences in Exercise 1 are true for you?**

Listening

3 **Listen to three people talk about traveling to work and school and complete the chart.**

Speaker	How does he/she get there?	How long does the trip take?	How does he/she feel about the trip?
1			
2			
3			

Reading

4 *PAIRS.* **Look at the photos and the title of the article. What do you think the article will say about Tadao Masuda, the man in the smaller picture?**

5 **Read the article and answer these questions.**

1. How long does Tadao spend traveling each day?
2. How does he feel about commuting?
3. How does he use the time on the train?

6 **Read the article again. Which of the sentences in Exercise 1 on page 64 are true for Tadao Masuda?**

Long-distance Commuter

So you think you have a difficult trip to work, with the traffic, heat, and mobs of people. You fight through crowds, down tunnels, up escalators. And you arrive at work sweaty and tired. However, it could be a lot worse.

Consider Tadao Masuda, who lives in Japan. His commute to work takes three and a quarter hours and then another three and a quarter back home again. He gets up at 4:00 A.M. Although he knows the commuting time to the minute, he leaves nothing to chance. He leaves at 4:55, gets on the train at 5:16, and always arrives in the office on time. He finally returns home at 8:50 in the evening, in time for dinner with his family. He knows his routine well—after all, he has been doing it for 30 years.

Despite not enjoying the trip, Tadao does not complain about it. "I don't actually enjoy commuting, but I definitely don't feel it is a waste of time. It is my private space, and I use this time for my own thoughts. I usually get home relaxed, despite the stress caused by a long day of hard work."

Today at age 65, he is considering a change. He would like to spend more time with his wife and family. In spite of staying with the same company all his life, he still gets only ten days off a year. However, will he be happy when he retires and ends his 30-year routine?

Grammar focus

1 **Study the examples of connectors. Notice the ways to express contrasting ideas.**

> You arrive at work tired. **However**, it could be a lot worse.
> **Although** he knows the commuting time to the minute, he leaves nothing to chance.
> I usually get home relaxed, **despite** the stress caused by a long day of hard work.
> **Despite** living only 10 miles from school, I have a pretty long commute.
> **Despite not** enjoying the trip, he doesn't complain about it.
> **In spite of** the noise and crowding, I'm glad I live in the city.
> **In spite of** staying with the same company all his life, he still gets only 10 days off a year.

2 **Look at the examples again. Complete the rules in the chart with *however, although, despite (not),* or *in spite of*.**

Connectors: *although, despite (not), however, in spite of*
Use __________ and __________ before a noun or gerund.
Use __________ before a gerund.
__________ is often followed by a comma, then a complete sentence.
Use __________ to introduce a subject + verb clause when there is another clause in the sentence.

Grammar Reference page 145

3 **Rewrite the sentences using the words in parentheses. Make any necessary changes.**

1. My commute is long. I enjoy living outside of the city. **(in spite of)**
   In spite of my long commute, I enjoy living outside of the city.
2. There was heavy traffic this morning. I got to work on time. **(despite)**
3. I don't really like my job. I need the money. **(however)**
4. I like my job. I don't like commuting. **(although)**
5. He is very busy. He manages to take some time off. **(despite)**
6. I leave on time. I'm always late. **(in spite of)**
7. He doesn't have an alarm clock. He always wakes up on time. **(despite not)**
8. I thought the interview went well. I didn't get the job. **(however)**
9. She works long hours. She has lots of energy. **(in spite of)**
10. It was raining hard this morning. I walked to work. **(although)**

Pronunciation

4 **Listen to the examples in Exercise 1 on page 66. Notice the position of the commas in the sentences. How do the commas affect the pronunciation?**

5 **Listen again and repeat.**

Speaking

6 *BEFORE YOU SPEAK.* **Look at the ideas in the notebook in relation to your time. How do you feel about each one?**

I have a long commute, and I don't enjoy it at all. The train is always crowded, so I never get a seat . . .

- Your commute
- Your home or family life
- The time you have for fun and relaxation
- Your work or school schedule

7 *PAIRS.* **Discuss your notes. Ask and answer follow-up questions.**

8 **Report to the class. Did you have any different attitudes toward time?**

Writing

9 **Write a note to a friend describing your regular trip to school or work. Use connectors in your answers to these questions.**

- How do you get there?
- What do you do while you're traveling?
- How long does it take?
- How do you feel about it?

Conversation to go

A: Although I try to be on time, I'm often late.
B: Maybe you should get a wake-up service.

Units 13–14

Unit 13 Going it alone

1 Imagine yourself in the following situations. Think about how you would feel and what you would do or might do if these things happened to you.

- You are at home alone, asleep in the bedroom. The sound of breaking glass in the next room suddenly awakens you.
- A friend is driving you back home from a late-night party. There are other people in the car. It's a long way, and you don't think the driver is in a good condition to drive.
- You have an important job interview tomorrow, and you want to be at your best. It's 1 A.M. and you can't get to sleep.
- Your family wants to take a vacation at a beautiful resort 600 miles away. The best way to get there is by plane, but someone in your family is terrified of flying.
- You've just moved into a new apartment. The people next door have lots of friends over all the time and they're loud and rude. The noise disturbs you and even keeps you from sleeping.
- You move to a new town where you don't know anyone. You have no friends or family nearby.

2 *PAIRS.* Take turns talking about how you would react to the situations in Exercise 1. Give reasons for your responses. How do your answers compare?

Unit 14 Commuter blues

3 Listen to the conversation between a husband and wife about a job offer he has gotten. How does the husband feel about it? What does the wife think?

4 *PAIRS.* Have a debate about the two sides in the conversation. Use *however, although, in spite of,* and *despite (not)* to show contrasting ideas.

Student A's position

- Family is important, but a good job is essential.
- The husband needs to make a living and build a career.
- Commuting is a problem, but the advantages of the job are greater than the disadvantages.

Student B's position

- Spending time with family is more important than a job.
- A long commute can be stressful and bad for your health.
- The husband has a good opportunity, but making money isn't the most important thing in life.

Review 1, Exercise 4
Student A

1. **You are a travel agent. Student B will ask you questions about Bangkok, Thailand. Use the information below to answer B's questions.**

   The best time for visiting Thailand is between November and February—during these months it doesn't rain so much, and it is not too hot. If you go to Bangkok, the worst two months are April, when it is extremely hot, and October, when it is very wet. Wear lightweight clothes. Casual clothing is fine except when you enter a temple. The Grand Palace, the Temple of the Golden Buddha, and the floating market are popular tourist attractions. You can shop all you want in Bangkok, including the night markets, where you can find inexpensive, good quality clothing and handmade crafts. Thai cooking is delicious, especially if you like spicy foods made with chilies, and you can find an amazing variety of exotic fruits. If you're interested, meditation study is very popular, as well as classes in Thai boxing, Thai cooking, and traditional massage.

2. **Now switch roles. You are the traveler and Student B is the travel agent who will answer your questions. You are planning to take a winter vacation in Colorado, U.S. Find out about:**

   - the best months to go
   - the weather and snowfall
   - winter sports and attractions
   - the scenery
   - what clothes to bring
   - other outdoor activities

Review 1, Exercise 5
Student A

Recipe: Scrambled eggs for two

4 eggs
1/4 cup milk
1 tablespoon butter
salt
ground pepper

In a small bowl, mix together the eggs, milk, and a pinch of salt. In a skillet, melt the butter over medium heat. Pour the egg mixture into the pan, stirring slowly. As the eggs begin to set (become less liquid), turn the heat up to high and shake the pan. Continue cooking and stirring occasionally until the eggs are set. Season with fresh ground pepper and serve.

Unit 16, Exercise 4
Student A

Look at your information and decide what questions you need to ask Student B in order to complete the information about Madonna. Student B will also ask questions.

A: When was Madonna born?
B: In 1958.

1. Madonna was born in __________ (when) in Bay City, Michigan, U.S.
2. She was named __________ (what) by her parents.
3. Her first recording contract was signed in 1982.
4. Her first big pop music recording, "Holiday," was released in __________ . (when)
5. Madonna's image as a Marilyn Monroe look-alike was introduced in her music video "Material Girl."
6. Her controversial song "Justify My Love" was banned by MTV because __________ . (why)
7. She was awarded a Golden Globe for her portrayal of Eva Peron in the movie *Evita*.
8. Today, the entertainer who is most admired by Madonna is __________ . (who)

Unit 22, Exercise 7
Student A

Ask Student B questions about these situations. First decide if the situation is possible or unlikely, then ask a question starting with:

What would you do if . . . ? OR
What will you do if . . . ?

- Your boss won't let you take a vacation for a year.
- You set up an appointment with an important client, then you remember you have a social appointment at the same time.
- Your best friend asks you for a ride to the airport at 5:00 tomorrow morning.
- You have a lot of homework tonight and you're exhausted.
- (Make up your own situation.)

Now switch roles. Student B will ask you questions, some of them possible, some hypothetical. Answer B's questions starting with:

I will (I'll) OR
I would (I'd)

Unit 7, Exercise 7
Student A

You are the director of Sweet Dreams—a big company that makes chocolates. You are going to have a meeting with a sales representative from a security company (Student B). Explain your problems (in the memo below) and see if he/she has any products that can help you. You have a budget of $20,000 to spend.

Our employees may be making long personal calls because our phone bill went up by 30 percent. Can you help me with this problem?

MEMO

- 30% increase in phone bills. Are employees making long personal calls?
- Two employees were robbed last week leaving work—no lights in the parking lot.
- 10% of chocolates disappear every week in the shipping department—maybe workers are eating them, but no evidence.
- Saw the sales manager playing computer games. How many others do this?

Unit 9, Exercise 6
Student A

Read the forecast. Decide whether you should have the beach party.

On Channel 11, they said that . . .

Channel 11 forecast
Have you noticed the dry air today? It's no surprise because bright sunshine and dry weather are coming in the next few days. This time the popular saying got it right—we expect good weather when there is no "r" in the month. After looking at my computers, I expect there will be warm and sunny conditions for the next few days.

Review 4, Exercise 7
Student A

Look at your information and decide what questions you need to ask Student B in order to complete the information about Venus and Serena Williams. Student B will also ask questions.

1. Venus Williams was born in June 1980.
2. Serena Williams was born in __________ .
3. When the girls were only three years old, they were taught to play tennis by their father, Richard.
4. They are managed and coached by their father.
5. Early in their careers they were called __________ by the press.
6. Venus's serve was recorded at 127 miles per hour—the women's world record.
7. __________ was defeated by Venus in the women's singles final to make Venus the Wimbledon 2001 champion.
8. In 2002 Venus was defeated by her sister Serena, the new Wimbledon champion.
9. __________ was honored as the 2003 Female Athlete of the Year at the annual ESPY awards.

Review 5, Exercise 9
Student B

Play the quiz game. Student A gives the answers first, then you identify *who, which, when, that, where,* or *whose*. Find the right clues below to help you.

- time of the day / begins to get dark then
- author / wrote the Harry Potter books
- state of the U.S. / once called the Sandwich Islands
- martial art / originated in Japan
- famous movie director / made thrillers
- place / beer is made
- sport / started in Scotland
- place in Egypt / you can see the Sphinx and the great pyramids there

Review 1, Exercise 4
Student B

1. You are planning to take a vacation in Bangkok, Thailand. Your partner, Student A, is a travel agent. Find out about:

- the best (and worst) times to go
- the weather
- other interesting things to do
- what to bring
- sight-seeing
- the shopping

2. Now switch roles. You are a travel agent. Student A will ask you questions about Colorado, U.S. Use the information below to answer A's questions.

Colorado is a magnificent place for a winter vacation, with some of the best skiing, snowmobiling, and snowboarding in North America. The mountain resorts get about 300 inches of snow a year, and it snows *somewhere* each month except August. Snowfall arrives early and stays late: many resorts are open from mid-October until June. There are ski slopes for every level, from expert to beginner, so it's perfect if you're taking the family. Bring your warm ski clothes and don't forget the sunblock if you don't want to get burned.

Love beautiful scenery but hate crowds? There are delightful mountain trails for hiking and camping, especially from June through October. Be sure to bring good hiking boots, insect repellent, and warm clothes for nighttime, when it can get pretty cool. Rocky Mountain National Park, sometimes called "America's Switzerland," has spectacular high-mountain landscapes. If you'd like to view wildlife such as deer, elk, and bighorn sheep, the best time is in late September and early October.

Review 1, Exercise 5
Student B

Recipe: Basic bean soup

1 pound dry beans
8 cups water
12 baby carrots
1 cup chopped onion
1/2 pound chopped ham
salt and pepper to taste

In a large bowl, combine the beans with the water. Cover and let them soak overnight.

In a large pot, over medium to high heat, combine the soaked beans with water, carrots, onion, and ham. Add more water to cover all the ingredients, if necessary. Bring to a boil, then reduce heat to low and simmer for 4 to 6 hours. Season with salt and pepper to taste and serve.

Unit 9, Exercise 6
Student B

Read the forecast. Decide whether you should have the beach party.

On Channel 12, they said that . . .

Channel 12 forecast
There's a saying that goes:

If salt is sticky and gains in weight,
it will rain before too late.

Well, for us today the picture is that a tropical storm from the south will bring hot and humid weather for the next couple of days. We will have scattered showers, especially in the morning. The temperature will remain high throughout the area.

Unit 16, Exercise 4
Student B

Look at your information and decide what questions you need to ask Student A in order to complete the information about Madonna. Student A will also ask questions.

A: When was Madonna born?
B: In 1958.

1. Madonna was born in 1958 in ___________ . (where)
2. She was named Madonna Louis Veronica Ciccone by her parents.
3. Her first recording contract was signed in ___________ . (when)
4. Her first big pop music recording, "Holiday," was released in 1983.
5. Madonna's image as a Marilyn Monroe look-alike was introduced ___________ . (where)
6. Her controversial song "Justify My Love" was banned by MTV because it was considered too shocking.
7. She was awarded a Golden Globe for ___________ . (what/for)
8. Today, the entertainer who is most admired by Madonna is Britney Spears.

Unit 5, Exercise 7
Student A

In each situation, the person underlined refers to your partner (Student B). Ask Student B for permission.

A: Can I use your computer?
B: I'm sorry, but I need it to do my homework.

1. Your computer isn't working and you want to check your email. Your roommate has a computer.
2. You're in a café. There are four of you, but there are only three chairs around the table. The person at the next table is alone and there are extra chairs around his/her table.
3. A friend is coming to visit you and is bringing a lot of luggage. Your sister/brother has a car. You want to borrow it so you can meet your friend at the airport.
4. You're on a train. The window is open and you're cold. There's a stranger sitting across from you.

Unit 5, Exercise 8
Student A

Listen to your partner. Use the cues to respond to Student B.

1. Give permission.
2. Refuse permission because you're trying to study.
3. Give permission.
4. Refuse permission because you left it at home.

Review 3, Exercise 7
Student A

You are the manager of an electronics superstore. You are looking for a new salesperson. Find out the following information from the person you interview:

- ☐ **past experience/responsibilities**
- ☐ **reason(s) for leaving previous job(s)**
- ☐ **experience in sales**
- ☐ **knowledge of electronics**
- ☐ **can work nights/weekends**
- ☐ **strengths/weaknesses**

Review 4, Exercise 7
Student B

Look at your information and decide what questions you need to ask Student A in order to complete the information about Venus and Serena Williams. Student A will also ask questions.

1. Venus Williams was born in June ___________ .
2. Serena Williams was born in September 1981.
3. When the girls were only ___________ years old they were taught to play tennis by their father, Richard.
4. They are managed and coached by ___________ .
5. Early in their careers they were called "Slice Girls" and "Sister Act" by the press.
6. Venus's serve was recorded at ___________ miles per hour—the women's world record.
7. Justine Henin was defeated by Venus in the women's singles final to make Venus the Wimbledon 2001 champion.
8. In 2002 Venus was defeated by ___________ , the new Wimbledon champion.
9. Serena was honored as the 2003 Female Athlete of the Year at the annual ESPY awards.

Review 5, Exercise 10
Student A

Now Student B gives the answers first, then you identify *who, which, when, that, where,* or *whose*. Find the right clues below to help you.

- master of Kung Fu / became a movie actor
- great Spanish artist / invented cubism
- sports / started in the U.S.
- boy / his nose grew longer whenever he told a lie
- name of currency / used in Canada and the U.S.
- place / you buy medicine there
- time / the day and night are the same length
- Chinese philosopher / started the religion of Confucianism

Unit 9, Exercise 6
Student C

Read the forecast. Decide whether you should have the beach party.

On Channel 13, they said that . . .

Channel 13 forecast
The satellite shows a very variable picture. The heavy rain that has been affecting the southern part of the country will be with us tomorrow. Many areas can expect winds and light showers. There will be a chance of fog—maybe even dense fog—in some areas. However, there are signs of good weather on the way.

Review 3, Exercise 7
Student B

You are interviewing for a job as a salesperson in an electronics superstore. Your partner (Student A), who is the store manager, will ask you questions. Use the following, in addition to your own information, to answer the questions:

Your last job was as a salesperson in a clothing store.
You left because the store went out of business.
You've had a few sales jobs as a student in the summer.
You love electronics; you have all the latest gadgets.
You can work nights but won't be able to work weekends.
You're responsible and creative, but not organized.

Review 5, Exercise 9
Student A

Play the quiz game. You give the answers first, then Student B identifies *who, which, when, that, where,* or *whose*.

Alfred Hitchcock	Giza	Judo
a brewery	Hawaii	golf
dusk	J. K. Rowling	

Review 5, Exercise 10
Student B

Now you give the answers first, then Student A identifies *who, which, when, that, where,* or *whose*.

Bruce Lee	the equinox	the dollar
Confucius	Pablo Picasso	Pinocchio
a pharmacy	basketball, baseball, and volleyball	

Unit 22, Exercise 7
Student B

Student A will ask you questions, some of them possible, some hypothetical. Answer A's questions starting with:

I will (I'll) OR
I would (I'd)

Now switch roles. Ask Student A questions about these situations. First decide if the situation is possible or unlikely, then ask a question starting with:

What would you do if . . . ? OR
What will you do if . . . ?

- You're in a meeting conducted in English and you don't understand everything.
- You have a job that you like, and another company offers you a better job.
- You're in an important meeting (or in class) and your cell phone rings because you forgot to turn it off.
- You are invited to dinner as a guest and they serve a food that you're allergic to.
- (Make up your own situation.)

Unit 5, Exercise 3
Students A and B

1. T
2. F
3. T (Even when invited, people may offer to pay for their meal, though no one expects the offer to be taken.)
4. T
5. T (It's OK to arrive up to 15 minutes late. As a general rule, guests shouldn't arrive early.)
6. F (You should ask permission first.)
7. F (Try to make eye contact with the server to get his/her attention.)
8. F
9. T
10. T (In fact, in most public places in the U.S., smoking isn't allowed at all.)
11. F
12. F

Unit 5, Exercise 7
Student B

Listen to your partner. Use the cues to respond to Student A.

A: Can I use your computer?
B: I'm sorry, but I need it to do homework.

1. Refuse permission because you need it to do homework.
2. Refuse permission because you're waiting for some friends.
3. Refuse permission because you need it to get to work.
4. Give permission.

Unit 5, Exercise 8
Student B

In each situation, the person underlined refers to your partner (Student A). Ask Student A for permission.

1. You are going to your friend's party, and you would like to stay overnight because the last train home is at 11 P.M.
2. You want to watch television. Your roommate is reading.
3. You need to leave class early because you have a doctor's appointment. Your teacher is very strict.
4. You are in an English class and you need a dictionary. You think your classmate has one.

Unit 27, Exercise 7
Students A and B

KEY: If you chose mostly . . .

a's: Lucky you! You are very cheerful and always look on the bright side of life! The future looks good.

b's: Cheer up and stop being so glum. Things aren't as bad as you think. Try to change your outlook a little.

c's: You are very level-headed and logical. There won't be any surprises for you tomorrow.

Unit 7, Exercise 7
Student B

You are a sales representative from Safe & Sound, a security company. Your products are listed below. You are going to have a meeting with the director of a chocolate company (Student A). First, find out his/her needs. Then try to sell your products. Remember to explain what the devices can do and what they can prevent.

A: Our employees may be making long personal calls because our phone bill went up by 30 per cent. Can you help me with this problem?
B: Yes, we can. We have something called "Call Stopper," which many companies use to stop long phone calls.

Safe & Sound
Product List

"Light Up"—a security light that comes on when it senses movement.	$1000
"Call Stopper"—a device that stops telephone calls to "unauthorized" numbers.	$600
"Micro Cam"—a tiny (2 in × 2 in) video camera.	$500
"Stop IT Now!"—latest technology to prevent computer users from using certain kinds of software (such as games).	$400

Unit 9, Exercise 7
Students A, B, and C

There was a mixture of sun and rain yesterday. The result was dense fog, which covered the region for 24 hours. Driving conditions were extremely dangerous and people were advised to stay home. The temperatures were low. But better weather is expected next week.

Unit 1

Present perfect with *yet, already, just*

- Use the present perfect to talk about things that happened in the past and have an effect on the present.
  *My neighbor **has** just **painted** his front door.*
  (It looks good now.)
  *Kim **has** already **written** her report.*
  (The report is finished now.)
- Use ***not yet*** when something has not happened but you expect it to happen or be completed in the future.
  *George hasn't finished that book **yet**.*
  (But he'll finish it in a few days.)
- Use ***just*** when the action happened very recently.
  *I've **just** washed the car.*
  (I finished washing it a few minutes ago.)
- Use ***already*** when the action is completed sooner than expected.
  *I've **already** cleaned up my desk.*
  (My desk is neat and clean now.)
- Use ***yet*** to ask whether something has happened that you are expecting will happen. ***Yet*** is used in questions and negative sentences.
  *Have you done your homework **yet**?*
  (Is your homework finished?)
  *I haven't finished **yet**.*
- ***Just*** goes between *have* and the past participle.
  *He has **just** cleaned the house.*
- ***Yet*** usually goes at the end of a clause.
  *I haven't walked the dog **yet**.*
- ***Already*** goes either between *have* and the past participle or at the end of the clause.
  *She has **already** bought some plants.*
  *She has bought some plants **already**.*

Note: You may also use the past tense with ***yet***, ***already***, and ***just***.
*Did you eat **yet**?*
*I **already** ate.*
*I **just** had breakfast.*

Unit 2

Real conditional

- Use the real conditional to talk about future possibilities.
  ***Will** I **need** rain gear **if** I **go** in June?*
- Use the real conditional to make suggestions and to give advice or warnings.
  ***If** you **plan** several flights, it **will be** cheaper to buy a pass.*
  ***If** you **book** your flight well in advance, you **may get** a better price.*
  ***If** you **use** sunscreen, you **won't get** sunburned.*
- The ***if* clause** states the condition (what needs to happen).
  ***If I have the time**, I'll help you with your homework.*
  (I will help you under the condition that I have time.)
- Use the simple present in the ***if* clause** and the future with *will* or *be going to*, a modal, or the imperative in the **result clause**.

If clause (condition): Simple present	Result clause: Future or imperative
*If you **go** to Australia,*	*you'**ll see** beautiful landscapes.*
	*are you **going to bring** me a souvenir?*
	*I **can lend** you a travel guide.*
	***take** me with you.*

- ***Unless*** means ***if not***.
  *Don't go to Australia **unless** you like hot weather.*
  (Don't go to Australia **if** you **don't** like hot weather.)

Note: The ***if* clause** can go before or after the result clause. Use a comma to separate the two clauses *only* when the ***if* clause** begins the sentence.
***If** you **use** sunscreen, you **won't get** sunburned.*
*You **won't get** sunburned **if** you **use** sunscreen.*

Unit 3

Count/non-count nouns and quantifiers

- Use these quantifiers with count nouns: ***a few***, ***a number of***, ***each***, ***few***, ***(not) many***, ***several***.
  *We need a **few** onions and **several** cloves of garlic.*
- Use these quantifiers with non-count nouns: ***a little***, ***a great deal of***, ***a little bit of***, ***much***, ***plenty of***.
  *Use a **little oil**. Don't add too **much flour**.*
- Use these quantifiers with both count and non-count nouns: ***all***, ***a lot of***, ***some***, ***any***, ***most of***.
  *Use **almost all the butter** and **all the potatoes**. Mix in **some onions** and **some salt**.*

Note: Use ***few*** (with count nouns) and ***little*** (with non-count nouns) to emphasize a lack of something. ***A few*** and ***a little*** mean a small quantity, but have a more positive tone.
*There are **few** good restaurants around here.*
(There aren't many good restaurants here—we need more.)
*There are **a few** good restaurants around here.*
(There are some good restaurants—we have a choice.)

Unit 4

Modals to talk about prediction and speculation

- Use ***will*** to talk about things that you think are very likely to happen in the future.
  *I'm sure interactive books **will** become very popular.*
  *People **won't** live on other planets.*
  ***Will** we still use cars?*
- Use ***may***, ***might***, or ***could*** to talk about possibilities in the future.
  *I think we **may** communicate entirely by email.*
  *We **might not** need telephones at all.*
  *Robots **could** be in every home in 50 years.*
- Use the **base form** of the verb (infinitive without *to*) after *will, may, might,* and *could.*
  *We will/may/might/could **win** the game tomorrow.*

Note: For some speakers, *may* expresses a higher probability than *might.*

Unit 5

Modals: *may, can, could,* and *Is it OK if . . . ?/Do you mind if . . . ?/Would you mind if . . . ?* for permission

- Use ***may***, ***can***, and ***could*** to ask for permission to do something.

***Can** I borrow your car?*	*No, I'm sorry. I need it.*
***Could** I use your cell phone?*	*Sure. Go ahead.*
***May** I leave early today?*	*Of course. / Sure.*

- Use the **base form** of the verb after *may, can,* and *could.*
  *May/Can/Could I **be** excused?*
- Use the **simple present** after *Is it OK if* + subject or *Do you mind if* + subject.
  *Is it OK/Do you mind if she **leaves** early today?*
- Use the **simple past form of the verb** after *Would you mind if* + subject.
  *Would you mind if she **left** early today?*
- The affirmative response to ***Do you mind if . . . ? / Would you mind if . . . ?*** is ***No, I don't*** or ***No, I don't mind.*** (It means "It's OK.")
  A: Would you mind if she left early today?
  *B: **No,** not at all.* (Meaning she has permission to leave early)
- Use ***Is it OK if . . . ?*** to ask permission in informal situations.
  A: Is it OK if I turn on the TV?
  B: Yes, of course.

Note: ***May*** is more formal than ***could***; ***could*** is more formal than ***can***.

Unit 6

Present perfect and present perfect continuous

- Use both the present perfect and the present perfect continuous to talk about recent actions and situations that have a result in the present.
- Use the present perfect when you focus on the result of a completed activity in the indefinite past.
  *He**'s tested** the power device and it works.*
  *I **haven't studied** for my exam—I think I'm going to fail.*
  ***Have** you ever **run** a marathon?*
- Use the present perfect continuous when you focus on an activity that may or may not be completed.
  *He**'s been testing** the power device.*
  I haven't been studying; I've been sleeping!
  Have** you **been running?
- Use ***have/has*** + **the past participle** to form the present perfect.
  *I **have seen** this movie before.*
  *She **has been** to my house several times.*
- Use ***have/has*** + ***been*** + **gerund** (verb + *ing*) to form the present perfect continuous.
  ***I've been playing** soccer for several years.*
- There are certain verbs that you can use in the present perfect but not usually in the present perfect continuous.
  *We**'ve known** each other since childhood.*
  *I know her face, but **I've forgotten** her name.*
  *How long **have** you **had** that car?*

Unit 7

Expressions of purpose

- Use expressions of purpose (***to, in order to, so that,*** etc.) to give reasons for an action.
  *Security companies are installing cameras **in order to** watch employees.*
  *Software is used **so that** they can record the websites you visit.*

Note the different forms:

to + **verb**
*They use cameras **to spy** on people.*

in order to + **verb**
*They use cameras **in order to spy** on people.*

so that + **subject** + **verb**
*They use cameras **so that they can spy** on people.*

in case + **subject** + **verb**
*They use cameras **in case someone steals** from the store.*

for + **verb** + ***-ing***
*They use cameras **for spying** on people.*

Unit 8

Past perfect

- Use the **past perfect** to talk about an action that happened before another action in the past.
  When I arrived at the terminal, the plane ***had*** *already* ***taken off****.*
  (First the plane took off, then I arrived at the terminal.)

- Form the past perfect with ***had*** + **the past participle**.
  The plane ***had left*** *when I arrived at the airport.*

- ***Already*** can go between *had* and the past participle or at the end of the sentence, for emphasis.
  He'd ***already*** *checked out of the hotel.*
  He'd checked out of the hotel ***already****.*

- Use time expressions, such as *by the time*, with the clause in the past tense when the other clause is in the past perfect.
  By the time *he* ***reached*** *the gate, his plane* ***had*** *already* ***left****.*

Note: There is a difference between the **past perfect** and the **simple past**.

When I **arrived** at the bus stop, the bus **left**.
(I arrived, and the bus left very soon afterward.)

When I **arrived** at the bus stop, the bus **had left**.
(The bus left; then I arrived.)

Unit 9

Indirect statements

- You can start indirect statements in two ways.
  1. **Subject +** ***told*** **+ object (+** ***that*****)**
     I told him that *I was ready to go.*
  2. **Subject +** ***said*** **(+** ***that*****)**
     I said that I was ready to go.

- When you report what somebody said, the verb tenses usually change.
  Simple present—simple past:
  "I'm ready to go."
  He said that he ***was*** *ready to go.*
  Simple past—past perfect:
  "We ***went*** *to the movies."*
  *They said they****'d gone*** *to the movies.*
  Present perfect—past perfect:
  *"I****'ve been*** *on vacation."*
  *She said she****'d been*** *on vacation.*

Note: There is no change with the past perfect.

"Anne ***had arrived*** *late, as usual."*
He said Anne ***had arrived*** *late, as usual.*

- The time expressions (*yesterday, this week*, etc.) often change with indirect statements.
  "I saw John ***yesterday****."*
  She said that she had seen John ***the day before****.*

- Possessive adjectives and pronouns usually change.
  *"****You*** *can use* ***my*** *dictionary."*
  He said ***I*** *could use* ***his*** *dictionary.*

Note: After *say* and *tell*, you don't need *that*.

Sang-Woo said that he was coming. OR
Sang-Woo said he was coming.

Sang-Woo told me that he was coming. OR
Sang-Woo told me he was coming.

Unit 10

Simple future and future perfect

- Use ***will/won't*** + **the base form** to say what you think will happen **at some point** in the future (simple future).
  I think we ***will wear*** *tiny computers on our wrists.*

- Use ***will/won't*** + ***have*** + **the past participle** to say that you think something will happen before a point in the future (future perfect).
  By the year 2150, *scientists* ***will have perfected*** *the "brainlink" computer.*

Unit 11

Indirect questions

- When you report questions that someone else has asked, the two types of questions are reported in different ways.

  1. ***Wh-*** **questions (*****who, what, where*****, etc.)**
     Subject + ***asked (me)*** **+ question word + subject + (modal verb) + main verb**

     "What's your date of birth?"
     She asked me what my date of birth was.

- Do not use question word order in the indirect question.
  X *She asked me what was my date of birth.*

  2. ***Yes/No*** **questions:**
     Subject + ***asked (me)*** **+** ***if*** **or** ***whether*** **+ subject + (modal verb) + main verb**

     "Can you work under pressure?"
     He asked me if I could work under pressure.

Note: With most indirect questions, *if* and *whether* usually mean the same thing. In other constructions (such as conditionals) they are not interchangeable.

- With indirect questions, the verb tenses usually change.
  "Do you like office work?"
  *He asked me whether I **liked** office work.*
  "Have you finished your work?"
  *He asked me if I **had finished** my work.*

Note: For more information about changes of tense in indirect statements, see Unit 9, page 144.

Unit 12

Narrative past tenses: simple past, past continuous, past perfect, past perfect continuous

- Use the past continuous:

  to describe longer actions and events in the past.
  *We **were working** last Monday.*

  to set the scene in a story.
  *The sun **was shining** and a breeze **was blowing** gently across the fields.*

  to talk about an action that was still going on when something else happened.
  *They **were waiting** in line when they saw each other for the first time.*

- Use the simple past to talk about completed activities in the past, often with a time reference (*yesterday, last year,* etc.)
  *Irene and Stella **grew up** on the same street.*
  *They **lived** there from 1990 to 1996.*

- Use the past perfect to talk about an activity that happened before another one in the past.
  *Mary dialed the wrong number because she **had written** it down incorrectly.*

- Use the past perfect continuous to talk about an activity that had been in progress before another one in the past.
  *The ground was wet. It **had been raining**.*

Unit 13

Present unreal conditional

- The form of the present unreal conditional is:
  If **+ subject + simple past tense form, subject +** ***would*** (or ***could*** or ***might***) **+ base form of the verb**

- Use the present unreal conditional to talk about unlikely or imaginary situations in the present and the future.
  ***If I had** a car, **I wouldn't take** the train every day.*
  (But I don't have a car, so I take the train.)
  ***Would you stop** working **if you won** the lottery?*
  (You probably won't win the lottery.)

- Use ***might*** or ***could*** instead of *would* when you are less certain.
  *If I **had** a lot of money, I **might** buy a boat.*

Note: Use ***were*** instead of ***was*** with all subjects, both singular and plural (*I, you, he, she, it, we, they*).
***If** I **were** rich, **I'd buy** a house abroad.*
***If** she **were** taller, she **could be** a model.*

Note: The ***if*** **clause** often goes first, but it can go second. When the ***if*** **clause** goes first, put a comma after it.
***If** I were rich, I'd be happier.*
*I'd be happier **if** I were rich.*

Unit 14

Connectors: *although, despite (not), however, in spite of*

- Use ***although, despite (not), in spite of,*** and ***however*** to introduce contrasting ideas.

  *Carolina didn't call Peter **although** she'd planned to.*
  ***Despite** going to bed very late, we got up at 6:00.*

- Note the different forms:

  despite or ***in spite of*** **+ noun** or **gerund**
  ***Despite an early departure**, we arrived late.*
  ***Despite leaving** early, we arrived late.*

  ***In spite of his health**, he climbed the mountain.*
  *He climbed the mountain, **in spite of being** in bad health.*

  despite not **+ gerund**
  ***Despite not having** an alarm clock, I manage to wake up early.*

  however **+ independent clause**
  *I often work long hours. **However**, **I enjoy the job**.*

  although **+ dependent clause** (subject + verb)
  ***Although I hate commuting**, I love my job.*

- Punctuation: dependent clauses or phrases starting with ***although, despite, in spite of*** at the beginning of a sentence use a comma to separate the two parts of the sentence. When the dependent clause comes at the end of the sentence, a comma is usually not needed.

  ***Although** I like my job, I don't like commuting.*
  *I don't like commuting **although** I like my job.*
  When ***however*** comes at the beginning of a sentence, a comma is often used.
  *I like my job. **However**, I don't like commuting.*

Irregular Verbs

Base form	Simple past / Past participle / Present participle
be	was (were) / been / being
become	became / become / becoming
begin	began / begun / beginning
break	broke / broken / breaking
bring	brought / brought / bringing
build	built / built / building
buy	bought / bought / buying
catch	caught / caught / catching
choose	chose / chosen / choosing
come	came / come / coming
do	did / done / doing
drink	drank / drunk / drinking
drive	drove / driven / driving
eat	ate / eaten / eating
fall	fell / fallen / falling
find	found / found / finding
fly	flew / flown / flying
forget	forgot / forgotten / forgetting
get	got / gotten / getting
give	gave / given / giving
go	went / gone / going
grow	grew / grown / growing
have	had / had / having
hear	heard / heard / hearing
keep	kept / kept / keeping

Base form	Simple past / Past participle / Present participle
know	knew / known / knowing
leave	left / left / leaving
lose	lost / lost / losing
make	made / made / making
mean	meant / meant / meaning
meet	met / met / meeting
put	put / put / putting
read	read / read / reading
ride	rode / ridden / riding
run	ran / run / running
say	said / said / saying
see	saw / seen / seeing
sell	sold / sold / selling
show	showed / shown / showing
sit	sat / sat / sitting
speak	spoke / spoken / speaking
spend	spent / spent / spending
take	took / taken / taking
tell	told / told / telling
think	thought / thought / thinking
throw	threw / thrown / throwing
understand	understood / understood /understanding
wear	wore / worn / wearing
win	won / won / winning
write	wrote / written / writing

Unit 1

clutter
contentment
energy
good health
good luck
happiness
productivity
stress
success
tension
tranquility
wealth

Unit 2

first-aid kit
hiking boots
insect repellent
money belt
rain gear
sleeping bag
travel guide
water bottle

Unit 3

basil
beer
butter
onions
pepper
salt
shrimp
stock

chili powder
garlic
ground beef
kidney beans
tomatoes
tomato paste
vegetable oil

add
(bring to a) boil
broil
chop
melt
mix
pour
sauté
serve
simmer
soak
stir

Unit 4

action figure
board game
cards
doll
erector set truck
handheld video game
jigsaw puzzle
remote-controlled car
skateboard
stuffed animal

Unit 5

blow your nose
eat with your fingers
have your elbows on the table
point at someone
put your feet up on the chair
reach across the table
slurp while eating
snap your fingers

Unit 6

achieve a goal/an objective
come up with an idea/a solution
develop a skill/a plan
invent a machine/a device
overcome an obstacle/a problem
pass an exam/a course
receive a certificate/an award
solve a problem/a puzzle
win a race/a prize

Unit 7

be accused of something
be convicted of something
be suspected of something
check on something or someone
commit a crime
deter someone
eavesdrop on someone
get away with something
keep an eye on something or someone
keep tabs on someone
look at something or someone
protect someone
restrict something
spy on someone
take advantage of something
uncover something

Unit 8

baggage claim
boarding pass
carry-on bag
check-in counter
duty-free shops
flight attendant
gate
luggage
runway
security checkpoint

Unit 9

cloud cover
clouds
fog
rain
showers
snow
sunshine
thunderstorms
tornado
winds

Unit 10

climb
decline
decrease
deteriorate
drop
fall
get better
get worse
go down
go up
improve
increase
rise
strengthen
weaken
worsen

Unit 11

experience
long-term goals
promotion
prospects
qualifications
references
strengths
weaknesses

Unit 12

afterward
at the same time
earlier
every time
previously
simultaneously
subsequently
whenever

Unit 13

cut off
fearful
isolated
jittery
jumpy
lonesome
petrified
scared
solitary
stressed out
tense
terrified

Unit 14

by the time
do something on time
in time for something
leisure time
a matter of time
spend time somewhere or with someone
take a long time
time off
a waste of time

Acknowledgments

The authors and series editor wish to acknowledge with gratitude the following reviewers, consultants, and pilots for their thoughtful contributions to the development of *WorldView*.

BRAZIL: São Paulo: Sérgio Gabriel, **FMU/Cultura Inglesa, Jundiaí;** Heloísa Helena Medeiros Ramos, **Kiddy and Teen;** Zaina Nunes, Márcia Mathias Pinto, Angelita Goulvea Quevedo, **Pontifícia Universidade Católica;** Rosa Laquimia Souza, **FMU-FIAM;** Élcio Camilo Alves de Souza, Marie Adele Ryan, **Associação Alumni;** Maria Antonieta Gagliardi, **Centro Britânico;** Chris Ritchie, Debora Schisler, Sandra Natalini, **Sevenidiomas;** Joacyr Oliveira, **FMU;** Maria Thereza Garrelhas Gentil, **Colégio Mackenzie;** Carlos Renato Lopes, **Uni-Santana;** Yara M. Bannwart Rago, **Associação Escola Graduada de São Paulo;** Jacqueline Zilberman, **Instituto King's Cross;** Vera Lúcia Cardoso Berk, **Talkative Idioms Center;** Ana Paula Hoepers, **Instituto Winners;** Carlos C.S. de Celis, Daniel Martins Neto, **CEL-LEP;** Maria Carmen Castellani, **União Cultural Brasil Estados Unidos;** Kátia Martins P. de Moraes Leme, **Colégio Pueri Domus;** Luciene Martins Farias, **Aliança Brasil Estados Unidos;** Neide Aparecida Silva, **Cultura Inglesa;** Áurea Shinto, **Santos:** Maria Lúcia Bastos, **Instituto Four Seasons. CANADA:** Stella Waterman, **Camosun College. COLOMBIA: Bogota:** Sergio Monguí, Rafael Díaz Morales, **Universidad de la Salle;** Yecid Ortega Páez, Yojanna Ruiz G., **Universidad Javeriana;** Merry García Metzger, **Universidad Minuto de Dios;** Maria Caterina Barbosa, **Coninglés;** Nelson Martínez R., **Asesorías Académicas;** Eduardo Martínez, Stella Lozano Vega, **Universidad Santo Tomás de Aquino;** Kenneth McIntyre, **ABC English Institute. JAPAN: Tokyo:** Peter Bellars, **Obirin University;** Michael Kenning, **Takushoku University;** Martin Meldrum, **Takushoku University;** Carol Ann Moritz, **New International School;** Mary Sandkamp, **Musashi Sakai;** Dan Thompson, **Yachiyo Chiba-ken/American Language Institute;** Carol Vaughn, **Kanto Kokusai High School. Osaka:** Lance Burrows, **Osaka Prefecture Settsu High School;** Bonnie Carpenter, **Mukogawa Joshi Daigaku/ Hannan Daigaku;** Josh Glaser, Richard Roy, **Human International University/Osaka Jogakuin Junior College;** Gregg Kennerly, **Osaka YMCA;** Ted Ostis, **Otemon University;** Chris Page, **ECC Language Institute;** Leon Pinsky, **Kwansei Gakuin University;** Chris Ruddenklau, **Kinki University;** John Smith, **Osaka International University. Saitama:** Marie Cosgrove, **Surugadai University. Kobe:** Donna Fujimoto, **Kobe University of Commerce. KOREA: Seoul:** Adrienne Edwards-Daugherty, Min Hee Kang, James Kirkmeyer, Paula Reynolds, Warren Weappa, Matthew Williams, **YBM ELS Shinchon;** Brian Cook, Jack Scott, Russell Tandy, **Hanseoung College. MEXICO: Mexico City:** Alberto Hern, **Instituto Anglo Americano de Idiomas;** Eugenia Carbonell, **Universidad Interamericana;** Cecilia Rey Gutiérrez, María del Rosario Escalada Ruiz, **Universidad Motolinia;** Salvador Castañeda, Alan Bond, Eduardo Fernández, Carla Silva, **Universidad Panamericana;** Raquel Márquez Colin, **Universidad St. John's;** Francisco Castillo, Carlos René Malacara Ramos, **CELE – UNAM/Mascarones;** Belem Saint Martin, **Preparatoria ISEC;** María Guadalupe Aguirre Hernández, **Comunidad Educativa Montessori;** Isel Vargas Ruelas, Patricia Contreras, **Centro Universitario Oparin;** Gabriela Juárez Hernández, Arturo Vergara Esteban Juan, **English Fast Center;** Jesús Armando Martínez Salgado, **Preparatoria Leon Tolstoi;** Regina Peña Martínez, **Centro Escolar Anahuac;** Guadalupe Buenrostro, **Colegio Partenon;** Rosendo Rivera Sánchez, **Colegio Anglo Español;** María Rosario Hernández Reyes, **Escuela Preparatoria Monte Albán;** Fernanda Cruzado, **Instituto Tecnológico del Sur;** Janet Harris M., **Colegio Anglo Español;** Rosalba Pérez Contreras, **Centro Lingüístico Empresarial. Ecatepec:** Diana Patricia Ordaz García, **Comunidad Educativa Montessori;** Leticia Ricart P., **Colegio Holandés;** Samuel Hernández B., **Instituto Cultural Renacimiento. Tlalpan:** Ana María Cortés, **Centro Educativo José P. Cacho. San Luis Potosí:** Sigi Orta Hernández, María de Guadalupe Barrientos J., **Instituto Hispano Inglés;** Antonieta Raya Z., **Instituto Potosino;** Gloria Carpizo, **Seminario Mayor Arquidiocesano de San Luis Potosí;** Susana Prieto Noyola, Silvia Yolanda Ortiz Romo, **Universidad Politécnica de San Luis Potosí;** Rosa Arrendondo Flores, **Instituto Potosino/Universidad Champagnat;** María Cristina Carmillo, María Carmen García Leos, **Departamento Universitario de Inglés, UASLP;** María Gloria Candia Castro, **Universidad Tecnológica SLP;** Bertha Guadalupe Garza Treviño, **Centro de Idiomas, UASLP. Guadalajara:** Nancy Patricia Gómez Ley, **Escuela Técnica Palmares;** Gabriela Michel Vázquez, Jim Nixon, **Colegio Cervantes Costa Rica;** Abraham Barbosa Martínez, Lucía Huerta Cervantes, Paulina Cervantes Fernández, Audrey Lizaola López, **Colegio Enrique de Osso;** Ana Cristina Plascencia Haro, Joaquín Limón Ramos, **Centro Educativo Tlaquepaque III;** Rocío de Miguel, **Colegio La Paz;** Hilda Delgado Parga, **Colegio D'Monaco;** Claudia Rodríguez, **English Key. León:** Laura Montes de la Serna, **Colegio Británico A.C.;** Antoinette Marie Hernández, **"The Place 4U2 Learn" Language School;** Delia Zavala Torres, Verónica Medellín Urbina, **EPCA Sur;** María Eugenia Gutiérrez Mena, Ana Paulina Suárez Cervantes, **Universidad la Salle;** Herlinda Rodríguez Hernández, **Instituto Mundo Verde;** María Rosario Torres Neri, **Instituto Jassa. Aguascalientes:** María Teresa Robles Cázares, **Escuela de la Ciudad de Aguascalientes / Universidad de Aguascalientes;** María Dolores Jiménez Chávez, **ECA – Universidad Autónoma de Aguascalientes;** María Aguirre Hernández, **ECA – Proyecto Start;** Fernando Xavier Gómez Orenday, **UAA – IEA "Keep On";** Felisia Guadalupe García Ruiz, **Universidad Tecnológica;** Margarita Zapiain B., **Universidad Autónoma de Aguascalientes;** Martha Ayala Cardoza, **Universidad de la Concordia / Escuela de la Ciudad de Aguascalientes;** Gloria Aguirre Hernández, **Escuela de la Ciudad de Aguascalientes;** Hector Arturo Moreno Díaz, **Universidad Bonaterra.**

WorldView 4 Student Audio CD

(This CD contains all the material for Student Books 4A and 4B.)

TRACK	STUDENT BOOK PAGE	WORKBOOK PAGE	ACTIVITY	
1			Audio Program Introduction	
2	3	14	Unit 1	Listening
3	5	14	Unit 1	Pronunciation
4	6	18	Unit 2	Pronunciation
5	7	18	Unit 2	Listening
6	11	22	Unit 3	Listening
7	13	22	Unit 3	Pronunciation
8	14	26	Unit 4	Listening
9	17	26	Unit 4	Pronunciation
10	23	32	Unit 5	Listening
11	25	32	Unit 5	Pronunciation
12	25		Unit 5	Pronunciation
13	25		Unit 5	Pronunciation
14	27	36	Unit 6	Listening
15	29	36	Unit 6	Pronunciation
16	30	40	Unit 7	Listening
17	33		Unit 7	Pronunciation
18	35	44	Unit 8	Listening
19	37	44	Unit 8	Pronunciation
20	41	50	Unit 9	Listening
21	43		Unit 9	Pronunciation
22	45	54	Unit 10	Listening
23	47	54	Unit 10	Pronunciation
24	49	58	Unit 11	Listening
25	51	58	Unit 11	Pronunciation
26	53	62	Unit 12	Listening
27	55		Unit 12	Pronunciation
28	55	62	Unit 12	Pronunciation
29	61	68	Unit 13	Listening
30	62	68	Unit 13	Pronunciation
31	65	72	Unit 14	Listening
32	67	72	Unit 14	Pronunciation
33	69	76	Unit 15	Listening
34	71		Unit 15	Pronunciation
35	71	76	Unit 15	Pronunciation
36	73	80	Unit 16	Pronunciation
37	73	80	Unit 16	Listening
38	78		Unit 17	Pronunciation
39	78		Unit 17	Pronunciation
40	79	86	Unit 17	Listening
41	83	90	Unit 18	Listening
42	85	90	Unit 18	Pronunciation
43	87	94	Unit 19	Listening
44	89	94	Unit 19	Pronunciation
45	90	98	Unit 20	Listening
46	91	98	Unit 20	Pronunciation
47	91		Unit 20	Pronunciation
48	99	104	Unit 21	Listening
49	101	104	Unit 21	Pronunciation
50	103	108	Unit 22	Listening
51	105	108	Unit 22	Pronunciation
52	106	112	Unit 23	Listening
53	109	112	Unit 23	Pronunciation
54	111	116	Unit 24	Listening
55	112		Unit 24	Pronunciation
56	112	116	Unit 24	Pronunciation
57	116	122	Unit 25	Listening
58	119		Unit 25	Pronunciation
59	119	122	Unit 25	Pronunciation
60	120	126	Unit 26	Listening
61	123	126	Unit 26	Pronunciation
62	124	130	Unit 27	Listening
63	127	130	Unit 27	Pronunciation
64	129	134	Unit 28	Listening
65	131	134	Unit 28	Pronunciation
66		40	Unit 7	Extra Pronunciation Practice
67		50	Unit 9	Extra Pronunciation Practice
68		50	Unit 9	Extra Pronunciation Practice
69		86	Unit 17	Extra Pronunciation Practice